German Grammar

by
Paul G. Graves, Ph.D.
University of Colorado

BARRON'S EDUCATIONAL SERIES, INC.

to my wife, Eva Alkalay Graves

All inquiries should be addressed to:
Barron's Educational Series, Inc.
250 Wireless Boulevard
Hauppauge, New York 11788

Library of Congress Catalog Card No. 89-17821
International Standard Book No. 0-8120-4296-4

Library of Congress Cataloging-in-Publication Data

Graves, Paul G.
  German grammar / by Paul G. Graves.
      p.   cm.
  "Adapted from Master the basics : German."
  ISBN 0-8120-4296-4
  1. German language—Grammar—1950- 2. German
language—Textbooks for foreign speakers—English. I. Graves,
Paul G. Master the basics : German. II. Title.
PF3112.G66   1990
438.2'421—dc20   89-17821
                                                            CIP

PRINTED IN THE UNITED STATES OF AMERICA

  56   550   987

Contents

Special Topics

Preface

This book is intended as a handy reference guide for high
school and college students as well as for businesspeople.
It should also be useful for those who have had some
German previously and want to "brush up" their grammar.
Nothing in the book has been taken for granted: every
term, every structural problem is explained clearly, con-
cisely, and "from scratch." Grammar, if it is to be the
indispensable helpmate of language study, should be pre-
sented in a friendly, nonthreatening way. This the author
has tried to do.

High school or college students need a grammar review
to serve them as a condensed, yet comprehensive, supple-
ment to their regular textbook. In this book they will find the
concise definitions and easy-to-grasp explanations that they
seek. Businesspeople, as well as others who want to
reinforce their knowledge of German, should find this book
a welcome tool.

For the orderly study of language, a minimum of grammar
is essential. Learning a language without grammar is the
way a child does it — by parrotlike imitation. Few adults are
comfortable going that route. Memorizing simple phrases
might be barely sufficient for casual travelers who want to
impress the natives with their smattering of German. In
many instances, though, the natives, in response, will try
out their English on the disappointed foreigner. Obviously,
even a very short conversational exchange requires a
minimal knowledge of grammar to structure a proper German sentence.

It is fortunate that the study of German offers no insu-
perable problems to the person whose native tongue is
English. The two languages, after all, are closely related;
many word forms and grammatical constructions can be
easily identified.

Paul Graves, Ph.D.
University of Colorado

How to Use This Book

In the chapters that follow, a numerical decimal system has been used with the symbol § in front of it. This was done so that you may find quickly and easily the reference to a particular point in basic German grammar when you use the index. For example, if you look up the entry "adjectives" in the index, you will find the reference given as §6. Sometimes additional § reference numbers are given when the entry you consult is mentioned in other areas in the chapter §.

The Basics

§1.

Pronunciation

§1.1 THE GERMAN ALPHABET

German Letter	Pronunciation
a	ah
b	bay
c	tsay
d	day
e	eh
f	ef
g	gay
h	haa (rhymes with baa)
i	ee (rhymes with sea or see)
j	yut (rhymes with shut)
k	kaa (rhymes with blah)
l	el
m	em
n	en
o	oh (as in no)
p	pay
q	koo
r	err
s	ess
ß	ess-tsett
t	tay
u	oo (rhymes with boo)
v	fow (as in fowl)
w	vay
x	iks (rhymes with six)
y	üpsilon
z	tsett

§1.2 VOWELS, UMLAUTS, DIPHTHONGS

A German vowel is long if it is followed by a single consonant or by ß (scharfes s) and another vowel, if it is doubled (*aa, ee, oo*), or if it is followed by a silent *h*.

Alphabet Letters	Sounds	Examples
a	Similar to the *a* sound in "father."	*Gābe* / gift *Strāße* / street
e	Similar to the *a* sound in "gate."	*Bēsen* / broom *gēgen* / against
i	Similar to the *i* sound in "mach*i*ne."	*Maschīne* / machine *Berlīn* / Berlin
o	Similar to the *o* sound in "bone."	*Ōfen* / oven *Bōden* / ground
u	Similar to the *oo* sound in "pool."	*Schūle* / school *gūt* / good
aa	Similar to the *aa* sound in "Saab."	*Sāāl* / hall *Wāāge* / scales
ee	Similar to the *a* sound in "share."	*Hēēr* / army *lēēr* / empty
oo	Similar to the *oa* sound in "road."	*Bōōt* / boat
ah	Similar to the sound in the exclamation "ah!"	*Bāhn* / railroad *Fāhrer* / driver
eh	Similar to the *ai* sound in "fair."	*sēhr* / very *Kēhle* / throat
ih	Similar to the *ea* sound in "team."	*īhm* / to him

Alphabet Letters	Sounds	Examples
oh	Similar to the o sound in "tone."	*Lōhn* / wage *Wöhnung* / apartment
uh	Similar to the e sound in "grew."	*Kūh* / cow *Hūhn* / chicken

Note: In this chapter only, the symbol ˉ above a vowel (ā) will be used to indicate a long vowel, and the symbol ˘ will be used to indicate a short vowel (ă).

When the vowel *i* is followed by an *e*, it is pronounced like *a* in the word *"leap."*

A German vowel is short if it is followed by more than one consonant or by a double consonant.

Alphabet Letters	Sounds	Examples
a	Similar to the o sound in "don."	*dănn* / then *hărt* / hard
e	Similar to the e sound in "belt."	*Fĕld* / field *hĕll* / clear
i	Similar to the i sound of "fins."	*Lĭnse* / lens *Lĭppe* / lip
o	Similar to the ou sound in "rough."	*ŏft* / often *Hŏffnung* / hope
u	Similar to the u sound in "bull."	*Mŭster* / sample *nŭll* / zero

The vowel *e* is short when it forms the suffixes -e, -el, -en, and -er or when it appears in the inseparable prefixes be-, emp-, ent-, er-, ger-, ver-, and zer-.

EXAMPLES:

Prefixes	Suffixes
běhandeln / to treat	*Fallě* / trap
ěmpfinden / to feel	*Himměl* / heaven
ěrobern / to conquer	*sehěn* / to see
gěgeben / given	*Litěr* / liter

An *umlaut* is the change in a vowel caused by partial assimilation to a succeeding sound. It is indicated by two dots above the vowel.

Umlaut	Sounds	Examples
ä	Pronounced like the short *e, as in* "bet."	*Länder* / lands *mächtig* / strong
ö	Similar to the *u* sound in "further."	*schön* / beautiful *förmlich* / formal
ü	There is no equivalent in English. Similar to the French *u*. Say *ee* with your lips in a whistling position.	*kühn* / bold *für* / for

Diphthongs are pairs of vowels.

Diphthong	Sounds	Examples
au	Identical to the *ou* sound in "ho*use*."	*Maus* / mouse *Faust* / fist
äu	Identical to the *oi* sound in "s*oi*l."	*Häuser* / houses *Säugling* / infant
eu	Pronounced like *äu*.	*Feuer* / fire *deutsch* / German
ai	Identical to the *i* sound in "p*i*ne."	*Hai* / shark *Mai* / May
ei	Identical to the *y* sound in "tr*y*."	*rein* / clean *breit* / wide

§1.3 CONSONANTS

The following German consonants should cause you no problems.

Alphabet Letters	Sounds	Examples
b	Identical to the *b* sound in "ball," *except* at the end of a syllable and before a consonant (see table below).	*Brücke* / bridge *beide* / both
d	Identical to the *d* sound in "day," *except* at the end of a syllable and before a consonant (see table below).	*dŭmm* / stupid *dänke* / thanks
f	Identical to the *f* sound in "fat."	*Fähne* / flag *frei* / free
g	Identical to the *g* sound in "gun," *except* at the end of a syllable and before a consonant (see table below).	*Gäst* / guest *Gäbel* / fork
h	Identical to the *h* sound in "here."	*Heim* / home *heiß* / hot
k	Identical to the *k* sound in "kick."	*Kätze* / cat *Köhle* / coal
m	Identical to the *m* sound in "moist."	*Milch* / milk *Männ* / man
n	Identical to the *n* sound in "nut."	*nĕtt* / nice *neu* / new
p	Identical to the *p* sound in "peace."	*Plätz* / place
t	Identical to the *t* sound in "tent."	*Teil* / part *tief* / deep
q	Identical to the *qu* sound in "queen." It is always followed by *u*.	*Quělle* / source
x	Identical to the *x* sound in "fox."	*Hĕxe* / witch

The following three consonants are pronounced differently at the end of a syllable or word and before a consonant.

Alphabet Letters	Sounds	Examples
b	Pronounced like *p* in "grape."	*Grāb* / grave *līeb* / dear
d	Pronounced like *t* in "rent."	*Hănd* / hand *Kīnd* / child
g	Pronounced like *k* in "dark."	*Lŏg* / log *sāgt* / says

The following consonants are pronounced in different ways, as explained in the table.

Alphabet Letters	Sounds	Examples
c	In foreign words before *e* or *ä*, it is pronounced like *ts* in "ha*ts*."	*Cäsar* / Caesar
j	Identical to the sound of *y* in "yes."	*Jăcke* / jacket *jěmand* / somebody
l	Should be pronounced with the tip of your tongue against the back surface of your upper front teeth. It should sound like the flat *l* in "William."	*Leute* / people *ält* / old
r	Can be rolled, the way the Scots do it; however, the uvular *r*, similar to the sound of gargling, is preferred.	*Reis* / rice *fěrtig* / ready
s	Before a vowel, *s* sounds like the *z* in "zoo."	*Sĩlbe* / syllable *sĩeben* / seven

Alphabet Letters	Sounds	Examples
ß	Ess-tsett, also called "scharfes *s*," is identical to the sound of *s* in "gas."	*Sträße* / street *Päß* / passport
v	Identical to the *f* sound in "*father*."	*Vögel* / bird *völl* / full
v	In words of foreign origin, it is identical to the *v* sound in "*very*."	*Villa* / villa *Väse* / vase
w	Identical to the *v* sound in "*veal*."	*Wëlt* / world *wö* / where
y	Sounds like the umlaut *ü*. If it occurs as the last vowel in a name, it is sounded like a long *i*.	*typisch* / typical *Ännÿ* / Anny
z	Identical to the *ts* sound in "*rats*."	*Zeitung* / newspaper *bezählen* / to pay

The following consonant combinations are pronounced in various ways, as explained in the table below.

Alphabet Letters	Sounds	Examples
ch	Identical to the *ch* sound in the name "Ba*ch*" or in the Scottish pronunciation of "lo*ch*"; occurs only after the vowels *a, o, u,* and the diphthong *au*.	*Säche* / thing *döch* / however *Tüch* / cloth *Rauch* / smoke
ch	Similar to the exaggerated *h* sound in "*humor*."	*Bëcher* / cup *Lïcht* / light

Alphabet Letters	Sounds	Examples
ch	In certain foreign words of French derivation, pronounced like *sh* in "*shoe*."	*chärmänt* / charming *chěf* / boss
ch	In certain words of Greek derivation, pronounced like *k* in "*keep*."	*Chäräkter* / character *Chīrürg* / surgeon
chs	Identical to the *x* sound in "*Mexico*."	*Ächse* / axis *Öchse* / ox
ck	Identical to the *ck* sound in "*black*."	*Säck* / sack, bag *Blick* / look
ph	Identical to the *ph* sound in "*phone*."	*Phräse* / phrase *phÿsisch* / physical
sch	Identical to the *sh* sound in "*shop*."	*Schläf* / sleep *schwärz* / black
sp	Pronounced like *shp* at the beginning of a word.	*Spīel* / game *spät* / late
st	Pronounced like *sht* at the beginning of a word.	*Stein* / stone *Stěrn* / star
th	Identical to the *t* sound in "*top*."	*Thrōn* / throne *Thēma* / theme

§1.4 STRESS

Boldface type will be used in this section to indicate stressed syllables. There is no written stress in German. Most dictionaries, however, do indicate stress, and it is recommended that you consult the dictionary when in doubt. Here are some general guidelines:

• In simple words of two syllables, the stress is usually on the first syllable.

EXAMPLES:
*Ga*bel / fork
*Win*ter / winter
*Wa*gen / wagon
*Er*de / earth

In compound nouns that consist of two or three words (see §4.2–3), the main stress is usually on the first word.

*Abend*luft / country air
*Pelz*tierzucht / fur farming
*Garten*werkzeuge / garden tools
*Lang*streckenläufer / long-distance runner

Separable prefixes are stressed most of the time.

EXAMPLES:
*ab*leiten / to derive
*an*sagen / to announce
*auf*stehen / to get up
*aus*sprechen / to pronounce
*bei*stimmen / to agree
*ein*richten / to arrange
*nach*geben / to give in

• The inseparable prefixes *be-*, *er-*, *ent-*, *ge-*, *ver-*, and *zer-* are never stressed.

EXAMPLES:
be*urteilen* / to judge
er*mahnen* / to admonish
ent*kommen* / to escape
ge*gangen* / gone
ver*dienen* / to earn
zer*brechen* / to break apart

• All nouns ending in *-ei* have the stress on the last syllable.

EXAMPLES:
Bäcke*rei* / bakery
Büche*rei* / library
Kondito*rei* / pastry shop
Metzge*rei* / butcher shop

- All verbs ending in *-ieren* have the stress on the next-to-the last syllable.

  EXAMPLES:
  studieren / to study
  trainieren / to train
  telefonieren / to phone

- Abbreviations are usually stressed on the last syllable.

  EXAMPLES:
  das ABC / the ABC
  das UK / the UK
  die UdSSR / the USSR
  die USA / the USA
  die UNO / the UN

2

Orthography

Orthography is defined as the art of writing words with the proper letters according to standard usage. It includes topics such as spelling, punctuation, capitalization, and syllabication.

To spell German correctly should pose no major problem since the language is highly phonetic. Every sound has its own fixed symbol, with but few exceptions — e.g., the mute letters *h* (as in *Bohne* / bean) or *e* (as in *dienen* / to serve). Mastering German pronunciation (Chapter 1) is a good way to learn German spelling. When in doubt, consult a dictionary.

What we are mainly concerned with in this chapter are those parts of orthography where German deviates from the rules that govern English usage.

2.1 CAPITALIZATION

German conventions on capitalization differ from English in several respects. Here are some guidelines.

All nouns are capitalized.

der Bruder / the brother
der Freund / the friend
der Mantel / the overcoat
die Zeitung / the newspaper
das Messer / the knife

Adjectives and other parts of speech that are used as nouns are capitalized.

das Neue / the new (one)
das Schöne / the beautiful (thing)
das gewisse Etwas / that certain something

- Adjectives that follow an indefinite pronoun (*jedes, etwas, wenig, viel,* etc.) are capitalized.

    jedes Schlechte / everything bad
    etwas Großes / something big
    wenig Schönes / little that is beautiful
    viel Wichtiges / much that is important

- Pronouns in letters used in the familiar form of address are capitalized.

    *Ich hoffe, daß **Du** das Paket erhalten hast.* / I hope that **you** have received the package.

- Pronouns used in the polite form of address are always capitalized.

    *Ich habe **Sie** dort gesehen.* / I have seen **you** there.
    *Wir haben **Ihnen** geschrieben.* / We wrote **you**.
    *Wie geht es **Ihrer** Schwester?* / How is **your** sister?

- The pronoun *ich* (I) is capitalized only if it stands at the beginning of a sentence.

- Adjectives of nationality are not capitalized.

    der deutsche Außenminister / the German foreign minister
    das französische Parfüm / the French perfume

§2.2 SYLLABICATION

Syllabication is the method by which words are divided in syllables. It becomes important mainly at the end of a line written communication.

Here are a few guidelines for dividing German words:

- Single vowels are never separated.

    EXAMPLES:
    aber / but NOT *a-ber*
    Fa-mi-lie / family NOT *Fa-mi-li-e*

- Diphthongs are treated like single vowels.

EXAMPLES:
Reue / repentance NOT Reu-e
euer / your NOT eu-er

A single consonant is transferred to the next syllable.

EXAMPLES:
se-hen / to see
Na-se / nose
ge-ge-ben / given

The letters *ch, sch,* and *ß* are considered single sounds whose components cannot be separated.

EXAMPLES:
Fä-cher / fans
ra-scher / faster
Stra-ßen / streets

If there are two or more consonants, the last of them starts the syllable that follows.

EXAMPLES:
Wän-de / walls
Rat-te / rat
Ent-set-zen / horror

The letters *ck* are separated into *k-k.* Thus *Bäcker* (baker) becomes *Bäk-ker.*

The letters *st* are never separated into *s* and *t.*

EXAMPLES:
Fe-ste / feasts
sech-ste / sixth

BUT

Ge-burts-tag / birthday

Note: *Tag* is a word in its own right, a component within a compound word (see §4.2 – 3), and the *s* belongs to the first word, having been added as a linking or connective letter.

§2.3 PUNCTUATION

German has the same punctuation marks as English, but the rules governing punctuation differ from the English in some respects. Here are some of the main differences:

- In German, a period is used after ordinal numbers.

  EXAMPLES:
  Freitag, den 5. Juli / Friday, July 5
  Ludwig XVI. / Louis XVI

- Independent clauses are set off by commas if they have different subjects and verbs.

  EXAMPLES:
  Paul las, und Edith schlief. / Paul read, and Edith slept.

  BUT

  Paul studierte und hörte dem Radio zu. / Paul studied and listened to the radio.

- Dependent clauses are always set off by commas.

  EXAMPLE:
  Das Hemd, das du trägst, kostet 20 Mark. / The shirt that you're wearing costs 20 marks.

- Any phrase that contains *zu, um zu, ohne zu,* or *anstatt zu,* is set off by a comma.

  *Es ist wichtig, ihn mit**zu**nehmen.* / It is important to take him along.
  *Sie ging ins Theater, **um** "Hamlet" **zu** sehen.* / She went to the theater to see "Hamlet."

- The last item in a series is *not* set off by a comma.

  Er studierte Englisch, Französisch und Russisch. / He studied English, French, and Russian.

- In German the exclamation mark is used much more frequently than in English. For instance, it is used after a command, an emotive expression, or when beginning a letter

EXAMPLES:

Einfahrt verboten! / Do not enter!
Schön, dich wiederzusehen! / Nice to see you again.
Das ist großartig! / That's great!
Lieber Paul! / Dear Paul,

Instead of an exclamation mark, a comma may be used to begin a letter, in which case the body of the letter begins with a lower-case letter.

Liebe Eltern, ich habe Euren Brief gestern erhalten. / Dear parents, I received your letter yesterday.

Word Order

§3.1 WHAT IS A SENTENCE?

A *sentence* is an organized group of words that express a statement, a question, a command, a wish, or an exclamation. A sentence starts with a capital letter and ends with a period, a question mark, or an exclamation mark.

EXAMPLES:

Kurt liest ein Buch. / Kurt reads a book. (statement)
Liest Kurt ein Buch? / Does Kurt read a book? (question)
Kurt, lies das Buch! / Kurt, read the book! (command)

Sentences consist of two basic parts: a *subject* and a *predicate*.

- A *subject* is the sentence unit that originates the action or the condition indicated by the verb. The subject is the "who" or "what" the sentence is about. It is often the first element in a simple sentence.

    EXAMPLES:

    Hans spielt die Violine. / Hans plays the violin.
    ↑

    > subject =
    > *who* plays the violin

    Schnee bedeckt die Stadt. / Snow covers the city.
    ↑

    > subject =
    > *what* covers the city

However, the subject is not always the first element of the sentence. Other parts of speech may precede it.

EXAMPLES:

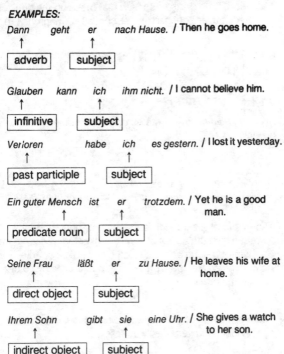

Dann geht er nach Hause. / Then he goes home.
↑ adverb — subject

Glauben kann ich ihm nicht. / I cannot believe him.
↑ infinitive — subject

Verloren habe ich es gestern. / I lost it yesterday.
↑ past participle — subject

Ein guter Mensch ist er trotzdem. / Yet he is a good man.
↑ predicate noun — subject

Seine Frau läßt er zu Hause. / He leaves his wife at home.
↑ direct object — subject

Ihrem Sohn gibt sie eine Uhr. / She gives a watch to her son.
↑ indirect object — subject

A *predicate* is that part of the sentence that expresses what is said about the subject.

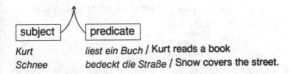

sentence

subject — predicate

Kurt   *liest ein Buch* / Kurt reads a book
Schnee   *bedeckt die Straße* / Snow covers the street.

- A subject must contain a noun (see Chapter 4) or pronoun (see Chapter 7); a predicate must include a verb (see Chapter 8). The parts of speech that make up the subject and predicate are defined and discussed in Chapters 4 to 11.

§3.2 TYPES OF SENTENCES ACCORDING TO FUNCTION

§3.2–1 Affirmative

An *affirmative sentence* states or affirms something in a positive way.

EXAMPLES:

Eva ist Deutsche. / Eva is German.
Dieser kleine Junge spielt Fußball. / This little boy plays football.
Alle unsere Freunde wohnen in München. / All our friends live in Munich.

The *object* of a sentence is the noun or noun phrase toward which the action of a verb is directed. A *noun phrase* consists of a noun accompanied by an article or adjective. An object can also be a pronoun that takes the place of a noun or a noun phrase.

- There are two types of objects: *direct* and *indirect*. These can be identified very easily as follows:

> A noun or noun phrase that follows the verb in the accusative is a *direct object*.

EXAMPLE:

Arthur liest die Zeitung. / Arthur reads the newspaper.

A noun or noun phrase that follows the verb in the dative (see §8) is an *indirect object*.

Karl schreibt dem Lehrer. / Karl writes to the teacher.

both the direct and indirect objects are nouns, the indirect ject usually precedes the direct object.

Karl schreibt dem Lehrer einen Brief. / Karl writes a letter to the teacher.

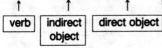

s not always necessary to have an object in a sentence.

Fritz studiert. / Fritz is studying.
Sie kommt morgen. / She is coming tomorrow.

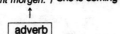

.2–2 Negative

German affirmative sentence can be made into a negative ntence by using the word *nicht* (not).

EXAMPLES:

Affirmative	Negative
Das war er. / That was he.	*Das war nicht er.* / That was not he.
Er ging in die Schule. / He went to school.	*Er ging nicht in die Schule.* / He did not go to school.

Here are some guidelines for the word order of *nicht* in a German sentence.

- *Nicht* precedes a predicate adjective, noun, pronoun, or adverb.

    EXAMPLES:
    Das Wetter war nicht schön. / The weather was not nice.
    Das ist nicht der Mann. / That is not the man.

- *Nicht* precedes a general time expression or a prepositic phrase.

    EXAMPLES:
    Er kam nicht oft. / He did not come often.
    Sie ist nicht zu Hause. / She is not at home.

- *Nicht* precedes past participles and infinitives.

    EXAMPLES:
    Er hat heute nicht gearbeitet. / He did not work today.
    Wir werden dich morgen nicht treffen. / We will not meet yc tomorrow.

- *Nicht* precedes separable prefixes.

    EXAMPLES:
    Ich hole dich morgen nicht ab. / I will not pick you up tomor
    Heute kommt er nicht zurück. / He will not come back today

- *Nicht* precedes the main verb in a dependent clause.

    EXAMPLES:
    Es ist möglich, daß er den Job nicht bekommt. / It is possib that he will not get the job.
    Wir gehen spazieren, wenn es nicht regnet. / We'll go for a walk if it does not rain.

- In a sentence with simple verb forms of the present or p tense, or if the entire sentence unit is to be negated, or fc special emphasis, *nicht* can stand at the end of the senter

EXAMPLES:

Franz gibt Karl das Auto nicht. / Franz will not give Karl the car.
Er gab es ihm nicht. / He did not give it to him.
Peter kommt leider nicht. / Unfortunately, Peter will not come.

Whenever two persons or objects are to be contrasted, *nicht* can precede any word that it negates, except the conjugated verb.

Nicht sie, sondern er kam heute zurück. / He, not she, came back today.
Nicht heute, sondern morgen ist sein Geburtstag. / His birthday is tomorrow, not today.

§3.2–3 Interrogative

In an interrogative sentence you ask a question. When you write it, you always put a question mark at the end. As in English, the subject follows the verb.

EXAMPLES:

Peter ist zu Hause / Peter is at home. (affirmative)
Ist Peter zu Hause? / Is Peter at home? (interrogative)
↑   ↑

| verb | subject |

Paul spielt Karten. / Paul plays cards. (affirmative)
Spielt Paul Karten? / Does Paul play cards? (interrogative)
↑ ↑

| verb | subject |

Interrogative sentences can also be formed by using interrogative pronouns or adverbs.

Welchen Film bevorzugen Sie? / Which film do you prefer?
Wie geht's? / How are you?

Use *nicht wahr?* to express the following:

> *Otto ist sehr nett, nicht wahr?* / Otto is very nice, isn't he?
> *Mein Bruder kauft ein Haus, nicht wahr?* / My brother is buying a house, isn't he?

§3.3 TYPES OF SENTENCES ACCORDING TO STRUCTURE

§3.3–1 Simple

A simple sentence has only one (main) subject and one (main) predicate.

§3.3–2 Complex

A complex sentence has one main clause and at least one subordinate, or dependent, clause. It still has a main subject and predicate.

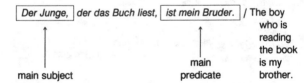

| Der Junge, | der das Buch liest, | ist mein Bruder. | / The boy who is reading the book is my brother. |

main subject   main predicate

Relative Clauses

A *clause* is a group of related words containing a subject and a predicate and is part of the main sentence. A *relative clause* is a subordinate clause introduced by a relative pronoun (see Chapter 7).

EXAMPLES:
<u>Main Sentence</u>
Der Junge ist mein Bruder. / The boy is my brother.
<u>Sentence to Be Changed into a Clause</u>
Der Junge liest das Buch. / The boy is reading the book.

Complex Sentence

Der Junge,	*der das Buch liest,*	*ist mein Bruder.*
↑	↑	↑
main subject	relative clause	main predicate

Please note that in the relative clause above (introduced by the relative pronoun *der*) the verb moved to the end of the clause.

Temporal Clauses

A *temporal clause* is introduced by a subordinating conjunction. A *conjunction* is a word that joins together sentences, clauses, or other words. The term *temporal* expresses a time relationship.

Als ich nach Hause kam, When I came home,	*war das Essen fertig.* the meal was ready.
temporal clause	main sentence

- As can be seen, the clause introduced by the subordinating conjunction *als* causes the verb *kam* to move to last place. Also, putting the temporal clause first causes inversion — that is, the placement of the verb before its subject in the main sentence.

- However, if we turn the sentence around, there is no inversion:

Das Essen war fertig, The meal was ready	*als ich nach Hause kam.* when I came home.
main sentence	temporal clause

• The rules outlined above also apply to the following examples.

Bevor / before	
Bevor er sie besuchte,	*kaufte er Blumen.*
Before he visited her,	he bought flowers
↑	↑
temporal clause	main sentence

Nachdem / after	
Nachdem ich ihn gegrüßt hatte,	*grüßte er mich.*
After I had greeted him,	he greeted me
↑	↑
temporal clause	main sentence

Seit(dem) / since	
Seit(dem) sie in Wien ist,	*hat er sie nicht gesehen.*
Since she has been in Vienna,	he has not seen her.
↑	↑
temporal clause	main sentence

Während / while	
Sie spielte Klavier,	*während er Zeitung las.*
She played the piano	while he read the paper.
↑	↑
main sentence	temporal clause

Other Types of Conjunctions

Obwohl / although	
Obwohl er nicht hungrig war,	*aß er sehr viel.*
Although he was not hungry,	he ate a lot.

weil / because	
Er bleibt zu Hause,	*weil er krank ist.*
He stays home	because he is sick.

§3.4 INCOMPLETE SENTENCES

In speaking, we do not always use complete sentences, that is, sentences that have a subject and a predicate. Quite frequently, one or the other part of a sentence is omitted, although it is clearly implied.

Complete Sentence	*Incomplete Sentence*

> *Wie geht's Ihnen? /*
> How are you?

Danke, mir geht's gut. / ↔ *Danke, gut /* Fine,
I'm fine, thank you. thanks.

> Wer spielt hier Klavier? /
> Who plays the piano here?

Mein Bruder spielt hier Klavier. / ↔ *Mein Bruder. /* My
My brother plays the piano here. brother.

> Wo ist deine Schwester? /
> Where is your sister?

Meine Schwester ist in der Schule. / ↔ *In der Schule. /* In
My sister is in school. school.

Parts of Speech

§4.

Nouns

§4.1   WHAT ARE NOUNS?

Nouns are words that label or name things (persons, objects, places, concepts, etc.). German nouns have endings that indicate their gender, number, and role within the sentence. All German nouns and words used as nouns are capitalized.

EXAMPLES:

Dieser Mann ist groß. / This man is tall.

Diese Frau ist klein. / This woman is small.

Diese Rosen sind schön. / These roses are beautiful.

There are two main types of nouns:

Proper nouns name a particular person, place, or thing.

> EXAMPLES
> *Herr Schmidt ist arm.* / Mr. Schmidt is poor.
> ↑

> *Anton ist glücklich.* / Anton is happy.
> ↑

> *Spanien ist interessant.* / Spain is interesting.
> ↑

Common nouns do not name a particular person, place or thing. They can be classified as *count* and *noncount*.

Count nouns refer to persons, places, or things that can be counted. They have both singular and plural forms.

> EXAMPLES:
>
> | Singular | Plural |
> |----------|--------|
> | *der Tisch* / the table | *die Tische* / the tables |
> | *die Uhr* / the watch | *die Uhren* / the watches |
> | *das Kind* / the child | *die Kinder* / the children |

Noncount nouns refer to persons, places, or things that cannot be counted; they usually have only a singular form.

> EXAMPLES:
> *der Zucker* / the sugar
> *die Butter* / the butter
> *das Mehl* / the flour

§4.2 GENDER

German nouns have three genders: masculine, feminine, and neuter. The gender of a noun is indicated by the definite article that accompanies it: *der* for masculine, *die* for feminine, and *das* for neuter. The grammatical gender does not always coincide with the biological gender. Furthermore, the gender of objects or of abstract nouns can be masculine, feminine, or neuter. Nouns, therefore, should be memorized along with their articles.

§4.2–1 Masculine, Feminine, and Neuter

● Nouns referring to human beings can be masculine, feminine, or neuter.

EXAMPLES:

Masculine	Feminine	Neuter
der Mann / man	*die Frau* / woman	*das Weib* / wife, woman
der Herr / Mr., gentleman	*die Dame* / lady	
der Sohn / son	*die Tochter* / daughter	*das Kind* / child
der Vetter / cousin	*die Kusine* / cousin	*das Mädchen* / girl
der Onkel / uncle	*die Tante* / aunt	*das Fräulein* / young lady, Miss
der Neffe / nephew	*die Nichte* / niece	*das Männlein* / little man

● Nouns ending in -*er* can also be masculine, feminine, or neuter.

EXAMPLES:

Masculine	Feminine	Neuter
der Vater / father	*die Mutter* / mother	*das Wetter* / weather
der Bruder / brother	*die Schwester* / sister	*das Wasser* / water
der Teller / plate	*die Butter* / butter	*das Zimmer* / room

Most nouns ending in *-en, -el, -ling,* or *-s* are masculine.

> EXAMPLES:
> *der Magen* / stomach
> *der Flügel* / wing
> *der Feigling* / coward
> *der Schlips* / tie

Most trees, flowers, and fruit are feminine.

> EXAMPLES:
> *die Tanne* / fir tree
> *die Eiche* / oak tree
> *die Rose* / rose
> *die Nelke* / carnation
> *die Banane* / banana
> *die Birne* / pear

> *EXCEPTIONS:*
>
> *der Apfel* / apple
> *der Pfirsich* / peach

● Nouns ending in *-age, -ei, -heit, -ie, -ik, -ion, -itis, -keit, -schaft, -tät, -ung,* and *-ur* are feminine.

> EXAMPLES:
> *die Garage* / garage
> *die Bäckerei* / bakery
> *die Weisheit* / wisdom
> *die Melodie* / melody
> *die Kritik* / criticism
> *die Operation* / operation
> *die Pleuritis* / pleurisy
> *die Menschlichkeit* / humanity
> *die Wissenschaft* / science
> *die Universität* / university
> *die Hoffnung* / hope
> *die Natur* / nature

- Nouns ending in *-ett, -il, -ium, -ma, -ment, -nis, -tel, -tum,* and *-um* (most of them of foreign origin) are neuter.

  EXAMPLES:

  das Ballett / ballet
  das Fossil / fossil
  das Stadium / stage
  das Klima / climate
  das Instrument / instrument

  das Hindernis / obstacle
  das Zehntel / tenth
  das Christentum / Christianit
  das Album / album

  > EXCEPTIONS:
  >
  > *der Irrtum* / error
  > *der Reichtum* / wealth

- Countries and cities can be masculine, feminine, or neuter.

  EXAMPLES:

Masculine	Feminine	Neuter
der Iran / Iran	*die Türkei* / Turkey	*das Spanien* / Spain
der Libanon / Lebanon	*die Schweiz* / Switzerland	*das Wien* / Vienna
der Sudan / Sudan	*die Normandie* / Normandy	*das Rom* / Rome

- Some masculine nouns referring to male persons have corresponding feminine nouns ending in *-in* that refer to female persons.

  EXAMPLES:

Masculine	Feminine
der Arbeiter / male worker	*die Arbeiterin* / female worke
der Sänger / male singer	*die Sängerin* / female singer
der Arzt / male physician	*die Ärztin* / female physician
der Student / male student	*die Studentin* / female studen
der König / king	*die Königin* / queen
der Graf / count	*die Gräfin* / countess

- Diminutives ending in *-chen* or *-lein* are neuter.

  These endings convey smallness or affection.

EXAMPLES:

Noun	Corresponding Diminutive
Paul	*Paulchen* / little Paul
Grete	*Gretchen* / little Grete
der Stern / star	*das Sternchen* / little star
die Maus / mouse	*das Mäuschen* / little mouse
das Bild / picture	*das Bildchen* / little picture
der Mann	*das Männlein* / little man
die Rose	*das Röslein* / little rose

§4.2–2 Nouns Having More than One Gender

There is a group of German nouns whose meaning depends
on gender, (determined by the definite article — see §5).
For example:
der Erbe is your heir who will inherit what you own.
das Erbe is the inheritance that he will inherit.

OTHER EXAMPLES:

Masculine	Feminine or Neuter
der Band / volume	*das Band* / ribbon
der Flur / corridor	*die Flur* / field
der Gehalt / contents	*das Gehalt* / salary
der Junge / boy	*das Junge* / offspring of an animal
der Kunde / customer	*die Kunde* / news
der Leiter / manager	*die Leiter* / ladder
der Schild / shield	*das Schild* / sign
der See / lake	*die See* / ocean
der Tau / thaw	*das Tau* / rope
der Verdienst / earnings	*das Verdienst* / merit

§4.2–3 Compound Nouns

By combining two nouns, compound nouns are formed. The
second noun of the compound noun determines the
gender. Two singular nouns may be joined to form a
compound noun, or a singular noun and a plural noun may
be joined.

Noun 1	Noun 2	Compound Noun
der Winter / winter	*der Mantel* / coat	*der Wintermantel* / winter coat
der Zahn / tooth	*die Bürste* / brush	*die Zahnbürste* / toothbrush
der Motor / motor	*das Boot* / boat	*das Motorboot* / motor boat
die Karten / cards	*das Spiel* / game	*das Kartenspiel* / card game
die Straßen / streets	*die Bahn* / railroad	*die Straßenbahn* / street car

Sometimes, compound nouns are joined together by the letter *s*.

Noun 1	Noun 2	Compound Noun
das Volk / people	*der Wagen* / car	*der Volkswagen* / people's car (VW)
der Frühling / spring	*das Fest* / festival	*das Frühlingsfest* / spring festival

§4.3 NUMBER

Number means that a word can be *singular* (referring to one person, thing, etc.) or *plural* (referring to more than one).

- We have briefly discussed the difference between count and noncount nouns. Here are some more noncount nouns that can be used in the singular only.

  EXAMPLES:
  das Wasser / water
  die Milch / milk
  das Salz / salt
  der Hunger / hunger
  der Durst / thirst
  der Reichtum / wealth
  die Gesundheit / health

- Some nouns occur only in the plural form. They refer to things that consist of more than one part.

EXAMPLES:
die Gliedmaßen / limbs
die Kurzwaren / dry goods
die Lebensmittel / food stuffs

● Other nouns are plural in German but singular in English.

EXAMPLES:
die Flitterwochen / honeymoon
die Möbel / furniture
die Ferien / vacation

● There are no definite rules for the formation of noun plurals.
The plural is recognized by the article or by the context.
The noun plural should be memorized along with the
singular. The plural article for all three genders is *die*. You
will find more about the formation of plurals on the following
pages.

§4.4   DECLENSION OF NOUNS

Declension relates to the endings of a noun that determine
its role within a sentence. *Case* is the inflectional form of a
noun indicating its grammatical relation to other words.

● The German noun has four cases: The *nominative*, marking
the subject of a verb; the *accusative*, or the direct object;
the *dative*, or the indirect object; the *genitive*, or the possessive.

EXAMPLE:

Der Hund The dog	*bringt* brings	*der Mutter* to the mother	*das Buch* the book	*des Mädchens.* of the girl.
subject ↕ nominative ↕ who?	verb	indirect object ↕ dative ↕ to whom?	direct object ↕ accusative ↕ what?	possessive ↕ genitive ↕ whose?

§4.4–1 Singular

Masculine nouns with the endings *-s* or *-es* in the genitive are called masculine 1 (strong). Those ending in *-en* in the accusative, dative, and genitive are called masculine 2 (weak).

Case	Masculine 1	Meaning	Masculine 2	Meaning
nom.	der Vater	the father (subj.)	der Junge	the boy (subj.)
acc.	den Vater	the father (obj.)	den Jungen	the boy (obj.)
dat.	dem Vater	to the father	dem Jungen	to the boy
gen.	des Vaters	of the father	des Jungen	of the boy

Neuter nouns have a genitive ending of *-s* or *-es* only.

Case	Noun	Meaning	Noun	Meaning
nom.	das Buch	the book (subj.)	das Geschäft	the business (subj.)
acc.	das Buch	the book (obj.)	das Geschäft	the business (obj.)
dat.	dem Buch	to the book	dem Geschäft	to the business
gen.	des Buches	of the book	des Geschäfts	of the business

Feminine nouns take *no* endings.

Case	Noun	Meaning	Noun	Meaning
nom.	die Katze	the cat (subj.)	die Frau	the woman (subj.)
acc.	die Katze	the cat (obj.)	die Frau	the woman (obj.)
dat.	der Katze	to the cat	der Frau	to the woman
gen.	der Katze	of the cat	der Frau	of the woman

Whether to use the *-s* or the *-es* as a genitive ending depends on the structure of the noun.

- For reasons of pronounciation, all nouns ending in sibilants (such as *-s*, *-ß*, *-sch*, *-z*, or *-zt*) take the *-es* ending.

Case	Noun	Meaning
nom.	*das Gas*	the gas
gen.	*des Gases*	of the gas
nom.	*der Ruß*	the soot
gen.	*des Rußes*	of the soot
nom.	*der Fisch*	the fish
gen.	*des Fisches*	of the fish
nom.	*der Arzt*	the physician
gen.	*des Arztes*	of the physician

The ending -*es* is preferred for nouns of one syllable, nouns with a stressed last syllable, or nouns ending with two or more consonants.

Case	Noun	Meaning
nom.	*der Tag*	the day
gen.	*des Tages*	of the day
nom.	*der Vertrag*	the contract
gen.	*des Vertrages*	of the contract
nom.	*der Kampf*	the fight
gen.	*des Kampfes*	of the fight

The shorter ending -*s* must be used if the noun ends in -*en*, -*em*, -*el*, or -*er*.

Case	Noun	Meaning
nom.	*der Wagen*	the car
gen.	*des Wagens*	of the car
nom.	*der Atem*	the breath
gen.	*des Atems*	of the breath

Case	Noun	Meaning
nom.	*der Kessel*	the kettle
gen.	*des Kessels*	of the kettle
nom.	*der Führer*	the leader
gen.	*des Führers*	of the leader

- The ending *-s* is preferred for nouns that end with an unstressed syllable.

Case	Noun	Meaning
nom.	*der Urlaub*	the vacation
gen.	*des Urlaubs*	of the vacation
nom.	*der Vortrag*	the lecture
gen.	*des Vortrags*	of the lecture
nom.	*der Abend*	the evening
gen.	*des Abends*	of the evening
nom.	*der Jüngling*	the young man
gen.	*des Jünglings*	of the young man

- The dative singular in masculine and neuter nouns of one syllable can take the optional ending of *-e*.

Case	Noun	Meaning
dat.	*dem Hund(e)*	to the dog
dat.	*dem Buch(e)*	to the book

§4.4–2 Plural

How do German plurals compare with their English counterparts? Almost all English nouns form plurals by adding -s or -es to the singular forms: girl, girls; house, houses. In German, there is a relatively small number of nouns that add -s to form the plural. Many nouns add various other endings, with or without an umlaut. Some plural forms do not change at all from the singular. As pointed out before, the only safe way is to learn the plural along with the genitive singular of the noun. If in doubt, consult a dictionary. In terms of forming plurals, most German nouns belong to one of five groups. Each group forms the plural endings in a different way.

Group 1

Nouns in Group 1 do not change in the plural, except for adding -n in the dative (unless the -n is there already). Some plural forms take the umlaut. Most of these nouns take the endings -chen, -lein, -el, -en or -er. They are mostly neuter or masculine.

Case	Singular	Plural	Meaning
nom.	*der Bruder*	*die Brüder*	the brother(s) (subj.)
acc.	*den Bruder*	*die Brüder*	the brother(s) (obj.)
dat.	*dem Bruder*	*den Brüdern*	to the brother(s)
gen.	*des Bruders*	*der Brüder*	of the brother(s)
nom.	*die Mutter*	*die Mütter*	the mother(s) (subj.)
acc.	*die Mutter*	*die Mütter*	the mother(s) (obj.)
dat.	*der Mutter*	*den Müttern*	to the mother(s)
gen.	*der Mutter*	*der Mütter*	of the mother(s)
nom.	*das Mädchen*	*die Mädchen*	the girl(s) (subj.)
acc.	*das Mädchen*	*die Mädchen*	the girl(s) (obj.)
dat.	*dem Mädchen*	*den Mädchen*	to the girl(s)
gen.	*des Mädchens*	*der Mädchen*	of the girl(s)

EXAMPLES:

der Onkel / uncle (accusative singular)   *Morgen besuche ich den Onkel.* / Tomorrow I'll visit the uncle.
das Fräulein / young lady (dative singular)   *Ich danke dem Fräulein.* / I thank the young lady.
der Mantel / coat (nominative plural)   *Wo sind unsere Mäntel?* / Where are our coats?
der Lehrer / teacher (dative plural)   *Er spricht mit den Lehrern.* / He talks with the teachers.

Group 2

Nouns belonging to Group 2 add *-e* (*-en* in the dative) to form plurals. Plural vowels sometimes take the umlaut. Most of these nouns — which may be masculine, feminine, or neuter — consist of one syllable.

Case	Singular	Plural	Meaning
nom.	*der Brief*	*die Briefe*	the letter(s) (subj.)
acc.	*den Brief*	*die Briefe*	the letter(s) (obj.)
dat.	*dem Brief*	*den Briefen*	to the letter(s)
gen.	*des Briefes*	*der Briefe*	of the letter(s)
nom.	*die Hand*	*die Hände*	the hand(s) (subj.)
acc.	*die Hand*	*die Hände*	the hand(s) (obj.)
dat.	*der Hand*	*den Händen*	to the hand(s)
gen.	*der Hand*	*der Hände*	of the hand(s)
nom.	*das Tier*	*die Tiere*	the animal(s) (subj.)
acc.	*das Tier*	*die Tiere*	the animal(s) (obj.)
dat.	*dem Tier*	*den Tieren*	to the animal(s)
gen.	*des Tieres*	*der Tiere*	of the animal(s)

EXAMPLES:

der Tisch / table (genitive singular) *Er sitzt am Ende des Tisches.* / He sits at the end of the table.
die Stadt / city (accusative singular) *Er besucht die Stadt.* / He visits the city.
der Hund / dog (dative plural) *Gib den Hunden Wasser!* / Give water to the dogs.
die Wurst / sausage (accusative plural) *Heute essen wir die Würste.* / Today we'll eat the sausages.

Group 3

Nouns in Group 3 add *-er* (*-ern* in the dative) to form the plural. As in Group 2, plural vowels (or diphthongs) sometimes take the umlaut. There are no feminine nouns in this declension.

Case	Singular	Plural	Meaning
om.	*der Mann*	*die Männer*	the man (men) (subj.)
cc.	*den Mann*	*die Männer*	the man (men) (obj.)
at.	*dem Mann*	*den Männern*	to the man (men)
en.	*des Mannes*	*der Männer*	of the man (men)
om.	*das Bild*	*die Bilder*	the picture(s) (subj.)
cc.	*das Bild*	*die Bilder*	the picture(s) (obj.)
at.	*dem Bild*	*den Bildern*	to the picture(s)
en.	*des Bildes*	*der Bilder*	of the picture(s)

Case	Singular	Plural	Meaning
nom.	das Haus	die Häuser	the house(s) (subj.)
acc.	das Haus	die Häuser	the house(s) (obj.)
dat.	dem Haus	den Häusern	to the house(s)
gen.	des Hauses	der Häuser	of the house(s)

EXAMPLES:

Das Buch / book (accusative singular)
Er liest das Buch. / He is reading the book.

das Kind / child (genitive singular)
Das ist der Ball des Kindes. / That is the child's ball.

der Wurm / worm (nominative plural)
Die Würmer sind in der Erde. / The worms are in the soil.

Gott / god (dative plural)
Sie beten zu den Göttern. / They pray to the gods.

Note: Nouns in Groups 1, 2, and 3 have the "strong" declension, in which the singular genitive takes an *-s* or *-es.* Some of the nouns take the umlaut. If in doubt about its proper use, please consult a dictionary.

Group 4

Nouns in Group 4 add *-n* or *-en* to the singular to form all four cases of the plural; they never take the umlaut. Most of these nouns are feminine. There are no neuter nouns in this group.

Case	Singular	Plural	Meaning
nom.	die Schule	die Schulen	the school(s) (subj.)
acc.	die Schule	die Schulen	the school(s) (obj.)
dat.	der Schule	den Schulen	to the school(s)
gen.	der Schule	der Schulen	of the school(s)
nom.	die Antwort	die Antworten	the answer(s) (subj.)
acc.	die Antwort	die Antworten	the answer(s) (obj.)
dat.	der Antwort	den Antworten	to the answer(s)
gen.	der Antwort	der Antworten	of the answer(s)
nom.	die Studentin	die Studentinnen	the female student(s) (subj.)
acc.	die Studentin	die Studentinnen	the female student(s) (obj.)
dat.	der Studentin	den Studentinnen	to the female student(s)
gen.	der Studentin	der Studentinnen	of the female student(s)
nom.	der Mensch	die Menschen	the human being(s) (subj.)
acc.	den Menschen	die Menschen	the human being(s) (obj.)
dat.	dem Menschen	den Menschen	to the human being(s)
gen.	des Menschen	der Menschen	of the human being(s)

Nouns ending with -in add -nen in the plural:

die Doktorin / woman doctor
die Doktorinnen / women doctors

Most masculine nouns in this group denote living beings:

der Junge / boy
der Elefant / elephant

This group has also been called the "weak" declension because of its -en endings. Masculine singular nouns add -en to form the accusative, dative, and genitive.

EXAMPLES:

der Held / hero (accusative singular)
Amerika ehrte den Helden. / America honored the hero.

EXAMPLES:

---

die Tante / aunt (dative singular)
Sie schuldet der Tante Geld. / She owes money to the
   aunt.

die Schwester / sister (nominative plural)
Die Schwestern spielen im Garten. / The sisters play in
   the garden.

der Bär / bear (dative plural)
Er fütterte einen von den Bären. / He fed one of the
   bears.

Group 5

The nouns in Group 5 are of foreign origin. Their declension
is similar to that of English nouns. They add the ending *-s*
to the singular to form the plural.

There is no *-n* ending in the dative plural. Nouns in this
group can be masculine, feminine, or neuter.

Case	Singular	Plural	Meaning
nom.	*der Park*	*die Parks*	the park(s) (subj.)
acc.	*den Park*	*die Parks*	the park(s) (obj.)
dat.	*dem Park*	*den Parks*	to the park(s)
gen.	*des Parks*	*der Parks*	of the park(s)
nom.	*die Kamera*	*die Kameras*	the camera(s) (subj.)
acc.	*die Kamera*	*die Kameras*	the camera(s) (obj.)
dat.	*der Kamera*	*den Kameras*	to the camera(s)
gen.	*der Kamera*	*der Kameras*	of the camera(s)
nom.	*das Radio*	*die Radios*	the radio(s) (subj.)
acc.	*das Radio*	*die Radios*	the radio(s) (obj.)
dat.	*dem Radio*	*den Radios*	to the radio(s)
gen.	*des Radios*	*der Radios*	of the radio(s)

EXAMPLES:

der Streik / strike (genitive singular) *Wegen des Streiks sind die Läden zu.* / Because of the strike, the stores are closed.
die Bar / bar (accusative singular) *Kennst du diese Bar?* / Do you know this bar?
das Kino / the movie theater (accusative plural) *Ich kenne alle Kinos in der Stadt.* / I know all the movie theaters in the city.
das Hotel / hotel (dative plural) *In diesen Hotels ißt man gut.* / One eats well in these hotels.

The following table summarizes the plural endings of nouns in Groups 1 through 5.

Group	Singular	Plural	Explanation
1	*der Löffel* / spoon *das Zimmer* / room	*die Löffel* / spoons *die Zimmer* / rooms	No plural endings
	der Vater / father *die Tochter* / daughter *das Kloster* / convent	*die Väter* / fathers *die Töchter* / daughters *die Klöster* / convents	Plurals take the umlaut.
2	*der Hund* / dog *das Schaf* / sheep	*die Hunde* / dogs *die Schafe* / sheep	Plurals end in -e; no umlauts.
	der Zug / train *die Nacht* / night *das Floß* / raft	*die Züge* / trains *die Nächte* / nights *die Flöße* / rafts	Plurals end in -e and take the umlaut.

Group	Singular	Plural	Explanation
3	*der Leib* / body *das Ei* / egg	*die Leiber* / bodies *die Eier* / eggs	Plurals end in *-er;* no umlauts.
	der Gott / god *das Glas* / glass	*die Götter* / gods *die Gläser* / glasses	Plurals end in *-er* and take the umlaut
4	*der Junge* / boy *die Antwort* / answer *das Bett* / bed	*die Jungen* / boys *die Antworten* / answers *die Betten* / beds	Plurals end in *-(e)n;* no umlauts.
5	*der Job* / job *die Bar* / bar *das Echo* / echo	*die Jobs* / jobs *die Bars* / bars *die Echos* / echos	Plurals end in *-s;* no umlauts.

§4.4–3 Irregular Nouns

There are some irregular nouns that, according to their
plural endings *(-en)*, should belong to Group 4. They are
irregular because, instead of adding *-s, -es,* or *-en* to form
the genitive singular, they add *-ns* or *-ens.*

Case	Singular	Plural	Meaning
nom.	*das Herz*	*die Herzen*	the heart(s) (subj.)
acc.	*das Herz*	*die Herzen*	the heart(s) (obj.)
dat.	*dem Herzen*	*den Herzen*	to the heart(s)
gen.	*des Herzens*	*der Herzen*	of the heart(s)
nom.	*der Name*	*die Namen*	the name(s) (subj.)
acc.	*den Namen*	*die Namen*	the name(s) (obj.)
dat.	*dem Namen*	*den Namen*	to the name(s)
gen.	*des Namens*	*der Namen*	of the name(s)

EXAMPLES:

---

der Glaube / faith (accusative singular)
Er behielt seinen Glauben. / He kept his faith.

der Wille / will (genitive singular)
Es war ein Akt des Willens. / It was an act of will.

der Gedanke / thought (nominative plural)
Die Gedanken sind frei. / Thoughts are free.

4.4–4   Nouns with Mixed Declensions

The declension of these nouns is strong in the singular (the singular genitive ends in *-s* or *-es*), and it is weak in the plural (each plural ending is *-en*). There are no feminine nouns in this declension. Mixed-declension nouns do not take an umlaut.

Case	Singular	Plural	Meaning
nom.	*der Schmerz*	*die Schmerzen*	the pain(s) (subj.)
acc.	*den Schmerz*	*die Schmerzen*	the pain(s) (obj.)
dat.	*dem Schmerz*	*den Schmerzen*	to the pain(s)
gen.	*des Schmerzes*	*der Schmerzen*	of the pain(s)
nom.	*das Auge*	*die Augen*	the eye(s) (subj.)
acc.	*das Auge*	*die Augen*	the eye(s) (obj.)
dat.	*dem Auge*	*den Augen*	to the eye(s)
gen.	*des Auges*	*der Augen*	of the eye(s)

Also belonging to the mixed declension are many foreign words, derived from Latin or Greek, with the endings *-ma* or *-um* in the singular and *-en* in the plural.

Case	Singular	Plural	Meaning
nom.	*das Thema*	*die Themen*	the theme(s) (subj.)
acc.	*das Thema*	*die Themen*	the theme(s) (obj.)
dat.	*dem Thema*	*den Themen*	to the theme(s)
gen.	*des Themas*	*der Themen*	of the theme(s)
nom.	*das Datum*	*die Daten*	the date(s) (subj.)
acc.	*das Datum*	*die Daten*	the date(s) (obj.)
dat.	*dem Datum*	*den Daten*	to the date(s)
gen.	*des Datums*	*der Daten*	of the date(s)
nom.	*das Museum*	*die Museen*	the museum(s) (subj.)
acc.	*das Museum*	*die Museen*	the museum(s) (obj.)
dat.	*dem Museum*	*den Museen*	to the museum(s)
gen.	*des Museums*	*der Museen*	of the museum(s)

- Some foreign words ending in *-us* keep their ending in all four cases of the singular, but take the ending *-en* in the plural

Case	Singular	Plural	Meaning
nom.	*der Organismus*	*die Organismen*	the organism(s) (subj.)
acc.	*den Organismus*	*die Organismen*	the organism(s) (obj.)
dat.	*dem Organismus*	*den Organismen*	to the organism(s)
gen.	*des Organismus*	*der Organismen*	of the organism(s)
nom.	*der Rhythmus*	*die Rhythmen*	the rhythm(s) (subj.)
acc.	*den Rhythmus*	*die Rhythmen*	the rhythm(s) (obj.)
dat.	*dem Rhythmus*	*den Rhythmen*	to the rhythm(s)
gen.	*des Rhythmus*	*der Rhythmen*	of the rhythm(s)

EXAMPLES:

das Drama / drama (genitive singular)
Ich kenne den Inhalt des Dramas. / I know the meaning of the drama.

> *der Realismus* / realism (accusative singular)
> *Ich bewundere den Realismus dieses Romans.* / I
>   admire the realism of this novel.

> *das Museum* / museum (genitive plural)
> *Der Reichtum dieser Museen ist erstaunlich.* / The
>   wealth of these museums is amazing.

§4.5 THE SAXON GENITIVE

The Saxon genitive is an abbreviated form of the regular genitive; it can be used with proper names that have no endings in the accusative and dative.

The Saxon genitive is used by adding an *-s* to the proper name:

Pauls Haus / Paul's house

It can either precede the subject or follow it. In the latter case, the subject takes an article.

EXAMPLES

Michaels Vater / Michael's father
Evas Garten / Eve's garden
                OR
Der Vater Michaels / the father of Michael
Der Garten Evas / the garden of Eve.

Note that in German there is no apostrophe preceding the Saxon genitive ending *-s*.

Proper names preceded by the genitive articles *des* or *der* do *not* add the *-s*.

EXAMPLES:

Der Vater des Michael / the father of Michael
Der Garten der Eva / the garden of Eve

- Words indicating family relationships (except *Bruder* and *Schwester*) also can be used in the Saxon genitive.

  EXAMPLES:
  Onkels Schuhe / uncle's shoes
  Mutters Kleid / mother's dress

- Place names follow the same rules as proper names.

  EXAMPLES:
  Belgiens Hauptstadt / Belgium's capital
  Roms Ruinen / Rome's ruins
  OR
  die Hauptstadt Belgiens / The capital of Belgium
  die Ruinen Roms / The ruins of Rome

- The preposition *von* (of) is used instead of the Saxon genitive if the proper names end in *-s, ß, -x,* or *-z.*

  EXAMPLES:
  die Bauten von Adolf Loos / the buildings of Adolf Loos
  die Opern von Richard Strauß / the operas of Richard Strauß
  der Anzug von Max / the suit of Max (Max's suit)
  die Krawatte von Franz / the tie of Franz (Franz's tie)

- The preposition *von* plus the dative is used to avoid stilted phrases.

  EXAMPLES:
  die Gesundheit von vielen anderen / the health of many others
  Er ist ein Freund von dem (vom) Bruder des Direktors. / He is a
  friend of the brother of the director (of the director's brother)

When studying German nouns, it is strongly recommended that you memorize them along with their gender (*m.* for masculine, *f.* for feminine, *n.* for neuter), the genitive singular, and the nominative plural.

Dictionary Word	Gender	Genitive Singular	Nominative Plural	Meaning
Apfel	*m.*	-s	¨	Apfels, Äpfel
Stunde	*f.*	—	-n	Stunde, Stunden
Bild	*n.*	-es	-er	Bildes, Bilder

Most dictionaries will also give pronunciation, stress, and part of speech.

§5.

Articles

§5.1 WHAT ARE ARTICLES?

Articles are words placed before nouns (or their modifying adjectives) that permit us to differentiate among them in some way.

- Articles that refer to specific persons or objects are called *definite articles* (equivalent to the English "the"). Articles designating nonspecific persons or objects are called *indefinite articles* (equivalent to the English "a" or "an").

Definite	Indefinite
der Tisch / **the** table	*ein Tisch* / **a** table .
der braune Tisch / **the** brown table	*ein brauner Tisch* / **a** brown table

- In German the article, when used in the singular, indicates the grammatical gender of the noun (masculine, feminine, o neuter).

    der Zug / the train
    die Blume / the flower
    das Papier / the paper

- All articles agree with the nouns that follow in gender and number.

    der Mann / the man
    die Männer / the men

    Demonstratives will also be included in this chapter because there are striking similarities between them and the definite article.

5.2 THE DEFINITE ARTICLE

The *definite article* points to people, objects, or concepts that are known or have been defined.

FORMS OF THE DEFINITE ARTICLE				
Case	**Singular**			**Plural**
	Masculine	**Feminine**	**Neuter**	**All Genders**	**Meaning**
Nom.	der	die	das	die	the
Acc.	den	die	das	die	the
Dat.	dem	der	dem	den	to the
Gen.	des	der	des	der	of the

Here are some examples of how the different forms of the definite article are used in sentences:

Masculine Singular
Der Junge ist nett. / The boy is nice.
Ich sehe **den** Mann. / I see the man.
Er dankt **dem** Vater. / He thanks the father.
Hier ist das Buch **des** Mädchens. / Here is the girl's book.

Feminine Singular
Die Frau ist schön. / The woman is beautiful.
Ich treffe **die** Mutter. / I meet the mother.
Er gibt es **der** Schwester. / He gives it to the sister.
Hier ist das Auto **der** Tante. / Here is the aunt's car.

Neuter Singular
Das Kind ist gut. / The child is good.
Ich liebe **das** Wetter. / I love the weather.
Er hilft **dem** Mädchen. / He helps the girl.
Ich höre die Stimme **des** Fräuleins. / I hear the young lady's voice.

Plural
Die Zeitungen sind hier. / The newspapers are here.   *Er liest die Bücher.* / He reads the books.   *Wir danken den Freunden.* / We thank the friends.   *Hier ist das Haus der Studenten.* / Here is the students' house.

In German the definite article is used more often than in English.

- It is used with many abstract nouns.

  EXAMPLES:
  Die Natur ist schön. / Nature is beautiful.
  Das Schicksal ist grausam. / Fate is cruel.
  Der Tod ist tragisch. / Death is tragic.

- It is used whenever the noun has a collective or generalized meaning.

  EXAMPLES:
  Der Mensch ist sterblich. / Man is mortal.
  Die Liebe ist eine Himmelsmacht. / Love is a heavenly power.

- It is used when expressing familiarity with works of literature, music, or fictional characters.

  EXAMPLES:
  Ich habe den Hamlet ganz vergessen. / I totally forgot Hamlet.
  Sie hat gestern die Aida gesungen. / She sang Aida yesterday.

- It is used with proper names that are identified by an adjective.

  EXAMPLES:
  der kleine Paul / little Paul
  der dumme Hans / stupid Hans

- It is also used with certain geographical terms.

EXAMPLES:

Die Friedrichstraße ist in Berlin. / Friedrich Street is in Berlin.
Der Baikalsee ist in Sibirien. / Lake Baikal is in Siberia.

The definite article is used when expressing a date.

EXAMPLES:

Morgen ist der 10. März. / Tomorrow is March 10.
Frankfurt, den 4. Oktober 1986. / Frankfurt, October 4, 1986.

It is also used with weights and measures.

EXAMPLES:

Das kostet 20 Mark das Kilo. / That costs 20 marks per kilo.
Das ist 50 Mark den Meter. / That is 50 marks per meter.

§5.3 THE INDEFINITE ARTICLE

The *indefinite article* points to something that is unspecified
— a person or an object in the singular. There are no plural
forms.

FORMS OF THE INDEFINITE ARTICLE				
Case	Masculine	Feminine	Neuter	Meaning
nom.	*ein*	*eine*	*ein*	a, an
acc.	*einen*	*eine*	*ein*	a, an
dat.	*einem*	*einer*	*einem*	to a, to an
gen.	*eines*	*einer*	*eines*	of a, of an

The use of the indefinite article in German is quite similar to
its use in English. Here are some examples:

Masculine
Ein Junge spielt dort. / A boy plays there.
Er hat einen Wagen. / He has a car.
Ich telefoniere einem Freund. / I call a friend.
Das ist der Hut eines Mannes. / That is a man's hat.

Feminine
Eine Frau ist here. / A woman is here.
Er nimmt eine Pille. / He takes a pill.
Sie hilft einer Freundin. / She helps a girl friend.
Das ist der Name einer Firma. / That is the name of a firm.

Neuter
Ein Hotel ist um die Ecke. / A hotel is around the corner.
Karl gibt mir ein Glas. / Karl gives me a glass.
Er schreibt einem Kind. / He writes to a child.
Das sind die Schuhe eines Mädchens. / Those are a girl's shoes.

- The indefinite article is omitted after the verbs *sein* (to be) and *werden* (to become).

  EXAMPLES:
  Ich bin Deutscher. / I am a German.
  Mein Vater ist Ingenieur. / My father is an engineer.
  Er wird Arzt. / He becomes a physician.

- It is omitted after the conjunction *als* (meaning "as").

  EXAMPLES:
  Ich sprach mit ihm als Chef. / I talked to him as a boss.
  Ich war in Ägypten als Arzt. / I was in Egypt as a doctor.

- It is also omitted in certain phrases referring to the body.

  EXAMPLES:
  Er hat Bauchweh. / He has a stomachache.
  Sie hat Zahnschmerzen. / She has a toothache.
  Sie hat Temperatur. / She has a temperature.

§5.4 DEMONSTRATIVES

Demonstratives point to a person or thing that has been referred to previously. They specify whether someone or something is relatively near (the demonstratives "this," and "these") or far ("that" and "those").

DEMONSTRATIVES INDICATING "NEARNESS"					
	Case	**Masculine**	**Feminine**	**Neuter**	**Meaning**
S i n g u l a r	*nom.*	*der, dieser*	*die, diese*	*das, dieses*	this one, this
	acc.	*den, diesen*	*die, diese*	*das, dieses*	this one, this
	dat.	*dem, diesem*	*der, dieser*	*dem, diesem*	to this one, to this
	gen.	*dessen, dieses*	*deren, dieser*	*dessen, dieses*	of this
P l u r a l	*nom.*	*die, diese*	Same as masculine.		these
	acc.	*die, diese*			these
	dat.	*den, denen, diesen*			to these
	gen.	*deren, derer, dieser*			of these

The genitive forms of the demonstrative *der* (*dessen, deren,* and *derer*) are rarely used.

• *Der, die,* and *das* are the most frequently used demonstratives. Standing by themselves, they function as demonstrative pronouns:

   Der ist sehr nett. / This one is very nice.

• Preceding the noun, they function as demonstrative adjectives, and can be used interchangeably with *dieser*:

   Der (dieser) Mann ist sehr nett. / This man is very nice.

- When spoken, they take a strong stress. They differ from the definite article in all genitive forms (rarely used) and in the dative plural.

Demonstratives Used as Pronouns

Den muß ich sehen. / **This one** I must see.
Denen gebe ich Geld. / **To these** I give money.
Dem glaube ich nicht. / I do not believe **this one.**

Demonstratives Used as Adjectives

Diese (die) Frau ist schön. / **This** woman is beautiful.
Dieser (der) Junge ist mein Bruder. / **This** boy is my brother.
Diesen (den) Studenten kenne ich. / I know **this** student.

- The neuter form of *dieser* may be shortened to *dies:*

  Dies ist ein schönes Kleid. / This is a beautiful dress.
  Dies Buch ist sehr gut. / This book is very good.

DEMONSTRATIVES INDICATING "FARTHER AWAY"

	Case	Masculine	Feminine	Neuter	Meaning
S i n g u l a r	nom.	jener	jene	jenes	that one, that
	acc.	jenen	jene	jenes	that one, that
	dat.	jenem	jener	jenem	to that one, to that
	gen.	jenes	jener	jenes	of that one, of that

DEMONSTRATIVES INDICATING "FARTHER AWAY"					
	Case	**Masculine**	**Feminine**	**Neuter**	**Meaning**
P l u r a l	*nom.*	*jene*			those
	acc.	*jene*	Same as masculine.		those
	dat.	*jenen*			to those
	gen.	*jener*			of those

EXAMPLES:

jener Mann / that man
jenes Kind / that child
jene Frau / that woman
jenen Leuten / to those people
jener Mädchen / of those girls
jene Personen / those persons

- *Dieser,* used as a demonstrative adjective (preceding a noun), corresponds in usage to both "this" and "that."

   an diesem Tag. / on this day OR on that day

- However, the meaning of *dieser* is restricted to "this" if it is contrasted to *jener* "that."

   Dieser Wein schmeckt besser als jener. / This wine tastes better than that one.

- Where there is no such contrast, *jener* expresses more remoteness than the English "that." It is not used very frequently.

§6.

Adjectives

Adjectives are words that describe or modify nouns. An adjective must agree with the noun that it modifies in gender and number.

das hübsche Kind / the pretty child
der nette Junge / the nice boy
die schönen Kleider / the beautiful clothes

§6.1 DECLENSION OF ADJECTIVES

§6.1–1 Weak Endings

If the adjective is preceded by words like *der* (the), *dieser* (this), *jener* (that), *jeder* (each), *welcher* (which), *solcher* (such), or *all(er)* (all), it takes the following "weak" endings:

Case	Singular			Plural
	Masculine	**Feminine**	**Neuter**	**All Genders**
nom.	-e	-e	-e	-en
acc.	-en	-e	-e	-en
dat.	-en	-en	-en	-en
gen.	-en	-en	-en	-en

Case	**Masculine Singular**	**Feminine Singular**
nom.	*der neue Hut* / the new hat	*die gute Frau* / the good woman
acc.	*den neuen Hut* / the new hat	*die gute Frau* / the good woman
dat.	*dem neuen Hut* / to the new hat	*der guten Frau* / to the good woman
gen.	*des neuen Hutes* / of the new hat	*der guten Frau* / of the good woman

Case	**Neuter Singular**	**Plural**
nom.	*das alte Radio* / the old radio	*die neuen Hüte* / the new hats
acc.	*das alte Radio* / the old radio	*die neuen Hüte* / the new hats
dat.	*dem alten Radio* / to the old radio	*den neuen Hüten* / to the new hats
gen.	*des alten Radios* / of the old radio	*der neuen Hüte* / of the new hats

EXAMPLES:

Ich mag den neuen Anzug. / I like the new suit.
Er dankt der guten Mutter. / He thanks the good mother.
Sie haßt die kalten Winter. / She hates the cold winters.
Ich bewundere das Talent dieses großen Dichters. / I admire the talent of this great poet.
Ich gehe spazieren an jedem schönen Tag. / I take a walk on each nice day.
Solches herrliche Wetter haben wir selten. / We rarely have such magnificent weather.
Welcher alte Mann sagte das? / Which old man said that?

§6.1–2 Strong Endings

If the adjective is *not* preceded by any of the words mentioned above, it takes "strong" endings.

Case	Singular			Plural
	Masculine	**Feminine**	**Neuter**	**All Genders**
nom.	-er	-e	-es	-e
acc.	-en	-e	-es	-e
dat.	-em	-er	-em	-en
gen.	-en	-er	-en	-er

Case	Masculine Singular	Feminine Singular
nom.	*alter Baum* / old tree	*frische Erde* / fresh soil
acc.	*alten Baum* / old tree	*frische Erde* / fresh soil
dat.	*altem Baum* / to an old tree	*frischer Erde* / to fresh soil
gen.	*alten Baumes* / of an old tree	*frischer Erde* / of fresh soil

Case	Neuter Singular	Plural
nom.	*junges Mädchen* / young girl	*alte Bäume* / old trees
acc.	*junges Mädchen* / young girl	*frische Rosen* / fresh roses
dat.	*jungem Mädchen* / to a young girl	*jungen Mädchen* / to young girls
gen.	*jungen Mädchens* / of a young girl	*neuer Bücher* / of new books

EXAMPLES:

Netter Junge, dein Sohn! / Nice boy, your son!
Schlechten Wetters wegen bleibt er zu Hause. / Because of the bad weather, he stays at home.
Er ist in großer Eile. / He is in a big hurry.
Sie ist guten Mutes. / She is of good cheer.
Ich liebe alte Sachen. / I love old things.

- Adjectives preceded by indefinite pronouns or numerals take strong endings:

andere gute Freunde / other good friends
verschiedene schöne Bücher / various beautiful books
viele neue Kleider / many new clothes
wenige alte Sachen / few old things
zehn kleine Kinder / ten little children
but: die zehn kleinen Kinder / the ten little children

EXCEPTION: when using *keine* and *alle,* the adjective following these indefinite expressions takes the weak endings:

keine neuen Kleider / no new clothes
alle guten Freunde / all good friends

§6.1–3 Mixed Endings

If the adjective is preceded by words like *ein* (a, one), *mein* (my, mine), *sein* (his), *ihr* (her), *kein* (no, none), *unser* (our), or *euer* (your), it takes the following endings:

	Singular			Plural
Case	**Masculine**	**Feminine**	**Neuter**	**All Genders**
nom.	*-er*	*-e*	*-es*	*-en*
acc.	*-en*	*-e*	*-es*	*-en*
dat.	*-en*	*-en*	*-en*	*-en*
gen.	*-en*	*-en*	*-en*	*-en*

Case	Masculine Singular	Feminine Singular
nom.	*ein neuer Hut* / a new hat	*eine gute Frau* / a good woman
acc.	*einen neuen Hut* / a new hat	*eine gute Frau* / a good woman
dat.	*einem neuen Hut* / to a new hat	*einer guten Frau* / to a good woman
gen.	*eines neuen Hutes* / of a new hat	*einer guten Frau* / of a good woman

Case	Neuter Singular	Plural
nom.	*ein altes Radio* / an old radio	*meine neuen Hüte* / my new hats
acc.	*ein altes Radio* / an old radio	*deine guten Frauen* / your good women
dat.	*einem alten Radio* / to an old radio	*seinen alten Radios* / to his old radios
gen.	*eines alten Radios* / of an old radio	*eurer alten Radios* / of your old radios

EXAMPLES:

Ich kaufe ihr einen neuen Hut. / I buy her a new hat.

Sie ist eine nette Frau. / She is a nice woman.

Er kommt mit einem neuen Radio. / He comes with a new radio.

Haben Sie keine neuen Zeitungen? / Have you no new newspapers?

Das sind die Puppen unsrer kleinen Mädchen. / These are the dolls of our little girls.

§6.1–4 Adjectives Used as Nouns

Whenever an adjective is used as a noun, it is declined like an adjective that precedes a noun.

Adjective	Adjective Used as Noun	Meaning
blond	*die Blonde*	the blonde
verwandt	*der Verwandte*	the relative
	ein Verwandter	a relative

- Adjectives used as nouns have the same endings whether preceded by *"der"* or *"ein"* words (see §6.1–1 and §6.1–3), *except* in the nominative masculine, the nominative neuter, and the accusative neuter of the *"ein"* words.

EXAMPLES:

Ich bringe der Blonden Blumen. / I bring flowers to the blonde.
Er ist ein Bekannter von mir. / He is an acquaintance of mine.
Das ist unser Neuestes. / This is our newest.

• Adjectives following words like *etwas* (something), *nichts* (nothing), *viel* (much), or *wenig* (little) take the neuter singular and are always capitalized.

EXAMPLES:

Er verspricht mir etwas Gutes. / He promises me something good.
Heute singt sie nichts Neues. / Today she sings nothing new.
Er wünschte ihr viel Gutes. / He wished her all the best.
Sie erzählte uns wenig Schönes. / She told us little that was nice.

§6.1–5 Predicate Adjectives

A *predicate adjective* stands after linking verbs like *sein* (to be), *haben* (to have), or *finden* (to find). It states something about the subject of the sentence. It never takes an ending.

EXAMPLES:

Die Schuhe sind teuer. / The shoes are expensive.
Die Frau wird alt. / The woman is getting old.
Er findet das Bild schön. / He finds the picture beautiful.

§6.1–6 Miscellaneous

• Adjectives ending in *-el* and *-er* lose the e when declined.

EXAMPLES:

dunkel / dark   *die dunkle Nacht* / the dark night
teuer / expensive   *der teure Schmuck* / the expensive jewelry

• The adjective *hoch* / high loses the c when declined.

der hohe Preis / the high price

§6.2 COMPARISON OF ADJECTIVES

§6.2–1 Comparative and Superlative

As in English, German adjectives have *comparative* and *superlative* forms. The comparative of an adjective is formed by adding *-er* to its stem (or *-r* if it ends in an e); the superlative is formed by adding *-st, or -est* if the adjective ends in *-d, -t, -s, -ß,* or z.

Adjective	Comparative	Superlative	Meaning
billig	*billiger*	*billigst*	cheap / cheaper / cheapest
leise	*leiser*	*leisest*	low / lower / lowest
gesund	*gesünder*	*gesündest*	healthy / healthier / healthiest
fett	*fetter*	*fettest*	fat / fatter / fattest
heiß	*heißer*	*heißest*	hot / hotter / hottest
kurz	*kürzer*	*kürzest*	short / shorter / shortest

- Adjectives ending in *-el* always shed the *e* in the comparative.

  dunkel, dunkler, dunkelst / dark / darker / darkest

- Many adjectives of one syllable take the umlaut.

Adjective	Comparative	Superlative	Meaning
alt	*älter*	*ältest*	old / older / oldest
arm	*ärmer*	*ärmst*	poor / poorer / poorest
grob	*gröber*	*gröbst*	coarse / coarser / coarsest
hart	*härter*	*härtest*	hard / harder / hardest
jung	*jünger*	*jüngst*	young / younger / youngest

Adjective	Comparative	Superlative	Meaning
kalt	*kälter*	*kältest*	cold / colder / coldest
klug	*klüger*	*klügst*	clever / cleverer / cleverest
lang	*länger*	*längst*	long / longer / longest
scharf	*schärfer*	*schärfst*	sharp / sharper / sharpest
schwach	*schwächer*	*schwächst*	weak / weaker / weakest
stark	*stärker*	*stärkst*	strong / stronger / strongest
warm	*wärmer*	*wärmst*	warm / warmer / warmest

A few adjectives have irregular forms.

Adjective	Comparative	Superlative	Meaning
groß	*größer*	*größt*	big / bigger / biggest
hoch	*höher*	*höchst*	high / higher / highest
nah(e)	*näher*	*nächst*	near / nearer / nearest
gut	*besser*	*best*	good / better / best
viel	*mehr*	*meist*	much / more / most

Comparative and superlative forms are used like any other adjectives, taking the identical endings.

EXAMPLES:

Höhere Berge sind schöner. / Higher mountains are more beautiful.

Das sind bessere Leute. / These are better people.

Das sind schärfere Messer. / These are sharper knives.

Mehr ist nicht immer besser. / More is not always better.

Er ist unser bester Student. / He is our best student.

London ist die größte Stadt, die ich kenne. / London is the largest city that I know.
Das ist mein jüngstes Kind. / This is my youngest child.
Wir lernen die schwersten Aufgaben. / We learn the hardest lessons.

- When the superlative is used as a predicate adjective, it takes a different form which does not vary in gender or number.

    EXAMPLES:
    Diese Kleider sind am teuersten. / These clothes are the most expensive.
    Diese Hemden sind am billigsten. / These shirts are the cheapest

§6.2–2 Positive

The *positive* degree is used to compare people or things of equal value.

    EXAMPLES:
    Ich bin (eben)so gescheit wie er. / I am just as smart as he.
    Er ist so groß wie ich. / He is as tall as I.

When comparing an inequality, the word **als** (than) is used.

    EXAMPLES:
    Ich gehe schneller als er. / I walk faster than he.
    Der Ring kostet mehr als die Uhr. / The ring costs more than the watch.

§6.3 Possessive Adjectives

There is a group of *possessive adjectives* that are actually possessive pronouns used as adjectives whenever they precede a noun:

> *mein* (my), *dein* (your), *Ihr* (your — formal), *sein* (his),
> *ihr* (her), *unser* (our), *euer* (your), *Ihr* (your — formal),
> *ihr* (their).

EXAMPLES:
mein Vater / my father
seine Mutter / his mother

ou will find a discussion of these forms in §7.2

§7.

Pronouns

A *pronoun* is a word that replaces a noun or a noun phrase, refers back to it, or inquires after it.

• Personal pronouns

> *Der Mann ist reich. **Er** ist auch freigebig.* / The man is rich. He is also generous.

The word *er* is a *personal pronoun;* it replaces the subject noun *Mann.*

• Reflexive pronouns

> *Der Junge wäscht **sich.*** / The boy washes himself.

The word *sich* is a *reflexive pronoun;* it refers back to the subject noun *Junge.*

• Possessive pronouns

> *Fritz liest **mein** Buch.* / Fritz is reading my book.

The word *mein* preceding the noun, is a *possessive pronoun* used as a *possessive adjective.*

> *Das Buch ist **mein.*** / The book is mine.

The word *mein,* standing by itself, is a *possessive pronoun;* it replaces the name of the possessor.

• Demonstrative pronouns

> *Dieser (der) Junge ist nett.* / This boy is nice

The words *dieser* and *der* are *demonstrative pronouns*, used as *demonstrative adjectives.*

> *Der ist nett.* / This one is nice.

The word *der,* standing by itself, is used as a *demonstrative pronoun;* it replaces the noun. Demonstratives were included and discussed in the section on Articles (see §5.4).

Relative pronouns

> *Das Mädchen, das dort steht, ist meine Schwester.* / The girl that is standing there is my sister.

The word *das* (the second *das*) is a *relative pronoun;* it refers back to the noun in the main clause.

Interrogative pronouns

> *Wessen Bleistift ist das?* / Whose pencil is this?

The word *wessen* is an interrogative pronoun; it inquires after a person or thing.

Indefinite pronouns

> *Hier darf man nicht rauchen.* / One must not smoke here.

In the sentence above, the word *man* is an indefinite pronoun; it replaces a noun subject, a person, or persons who are not clearly defined. *Etwas* / something, replaces a thing or an object. The different types of pronouns will be discussed in the sections below.

§7.1 PERSONAL PRONOUNS

Personal pronouns refer to living beings, objects, or ideas. The first person is used by a speaker or writer about himself or herself alone or with others (*ich, wir* / I, we). The second person is the person spoken or written to (*du, ihr, Sie* / you). The third person is the person or thing spoken or written about (*er, sie, es; sie* / he, she, it, they).

§7.1–1 Subject

Subject pronouns are used in the nominative. They have the following forms:

	Person	German Forms	English Equivalent	Examples
S i n g u l a r	1st	*ich*	I	*Ich bin zufrieden.* / I am satisfied.
	2nd	*du*	you (familiar)	*Lernst du Deutsch?* / Are you learning German?
		Sie	you (formal)	*Kommen Sie?* / Are you coming?
	3rd	*er*	he	*Er spricht gut.* / He speaks well.
		sie	she	*Sie ist nett.* / She is nice.
		es	it	*Es schneit.* / It is snowing.
P l u r a l	1st	*wir*	we	*Wir gehen weg.* / We go away.
	2nd	*ihr*	you (familiar)	*Wo seid ihr?* / Where are you?
		Sie	you (formal)	*Wo wohnen Sie?* / Where do you live?
	3rd	*sie*	they	*Sie sind hier.* / They are here.

- The pronoun *ich* (I) is never capitalized unless it is the first word of a sentence.
- The familiar forms *du* and *ihr* are used when addressing members of the family, children, or close friends.
- *Sie* (capitalized) is used in a more formal way; it is both singular and plural.

EXAMPLES:

Siehst du das, Mutter? / Do you see that, Mother?

Karl und Franz, habt ihr das Geschirr gewaschen? / Karl and
  Franz, did you wash the dishes?

Herr Schmidt, haben Sie das gelesen? / Herr Schmidt, did you
  read this?

Meine Herren, sind Sie damit einverstanden? / Gentlemen, do
  you agree with this?

7.1–2 Object

Object Pronouns in the Accusative

Object pronouns are used in the accusative as direct
objects or as objects of a preposition that takes the accusative. They have the following forms:

Person	German Forms	English Equivalent	Examples
1st	*mich*	me	*Karl ruft mich.* / Karl calls me.
2nd	*dich*	you (familiar)	*Er braucht dich.* / He needs you.
	Sie	you (formal)	*Wir besuchen Sie.* / We visit you.
3rd	*ihn*	him	*Eva liebt ihn.* / Eva loves him.
	sie	her	*Paul liebt sie.* / Paul loves her.
	es	it	*Hans mag es.* / Hans likes it.
1st	*uns*	us	*Sie sieht uns.* / She sees us.
2nd	*euch*	you (familiar)	*Kurt sieht euch.* / Kurt sees you.
	Sie	you (formal)	*Ich höre Sie.* / I hear you.
3rd	*sie*	them	*Nora wäscht sie.* / Nora washes them.

EXAMPLES:

Wo triffst du mich heute? / Where are you meeting me today?

Ich höre ihn sehr gut. / I hear him very well.

Wir sehen Sie morgen, Herr Schmidt. / We will see you
  tomorrow, *Mr. Schmidt.*

Ich liebe sie beide. / I love them both.

Hans besucht uns morgen. / Hans will visit us tomorrow.

Object Pronouns in the Dative

Object pronouns are used in the dative as indirect objects or as objects of a preposition that takes the dative. They have the following forms:

	Person	German Form	English Equivalent	Examples
S i n g u l a r	1st	*mir*	to me	*Karl kommt zu mir.* / Karl comes to me.
	2nd	*dir*	to you (familiar)	*Das gehört dir.* / That belongs to you.
		Ihnen	to you (formal)	*Otto schreibt Ihnen.* / Otto writes to you.
	3rd	*ihm* (m.)	to him	*Das Buch gehört ihm.* / The book belongs to him.
		ihr (f.)	to her	*Ich fahre zu ihr.* / I drive to her.
		ihm (n.)	to it	*Gib ihm (dem Pferd) Wasser!* / Give it (the horse) some water
P l u r a l	1st	*uns*	to us	*Paul spricht zu uns.* / Paul speaks to us.
	2nd	*euch*	to you (familiar)	*Schreibt euch das Kind?* / Does the child write you?
		Ihnen	to you (formal)	*Fritz fährt zu ihnen.* / Fritz is driving to you.
	3rd	*ihnen*	to them	*Er gibt ihnen das Geld.* / He gives the money to them.

EXAMPLES:

*Er gibt **mir** etwas.* / He gives me something.

*Er kommt zu **euch**.* / He comes to you.

*Das gehört **Ihnen**,* Herr Müller / That belongs to you, Mr. Müller.

*Das gehört **ihm**,* dem Sohn. / That belongs to him, the son.

*Das gehört **ihr**,* der Tochter. / That belongs to her, the daughter.

*Das gehört **ihm**,* dem Mädchen. / That belongs to her, the girl.

*Das gehört **ihm**,* dem Tier. / That belongs to it, the animal.

Note: The word *Mädchen* (girl) is a neuter noun.

7.1–3   Reflexive

A *reflexive pronoun* "reflects" or refers back to the subject:

Ich wasche mich. / I wash myself. German does not distinguish reflexive pronouns from object pronouns by the use of "self" (as we do in English). It uses the object pronouns in the accusative and the dative.

Reflexive Pronouns in the Accusative

Reflexive pronouns in the accusative take the same forms as the corresponding object pronouns, except in the second person formal and in the third person.

Person	German Form	English Equivalent	Examples
1st	*mich*	myself	*Ich rasiere mich.* / I shave myself.
2nd	*dich*	yourself (familiar)	*Du schneidest dich.* / You cut yourself.
	sich	yourself (formal)	*Sie schneiden sich.* / You cut yourself.
3rd	*sich*	himself	*Er verletzt sich.* / He hurts himself.
		herself	*Sie kämmt sich.* / She combs herself.
		itself	*Es (das Kind) wäscht sich.* / It (the child) washes itself.
1st	*uns*	ourselves	*Wir waschen uns.* / We wash ourselves.
2nd	*euch*	yourselves (familiar)	*Ihr kämmt euch.* / You comb yourselves.
	sich	yourselves (formal)	*Sie kämmen sich.* / You comb yourselves.
3rd	*sich*	themselves	*Sie kämmen sich.* / They comb themselves.

Some reflexive forms in German have nonreflexive forms in English.

> EXAMPLES:
>
> *Er fürchtet **sich** vor dem Donner.* / He is afraid of thunder.
> *Wir freuen **uns** auf Ostern.* / We look forward to Easter.
> *Ihr erinnert **euch** daran.* / You remember (remind yourself of) it.
> *Sie weigern **sich,** es zu tun.* / They refuse to do it.
> *Sie hat **sich** versprochen.* / She made a slip of the tongue.
> *Er hat **sich** verlaufen.* / He lost his way.
> *Ich habe **mich** erkältet.* / I caught a cold.

Reflexive Pronouns in the Dative

Reflexive pronouns in the dative take the same forms as corresponding object pronouns in the first person and second person familiar. In the second person formal and in the third person, they have the same form as reflexive pronouns in the accusative.

> EXAMPLES:
>
> *Ich gefalle **mir** sehr gut.* / I like myself very much.
> *Du hast **dir** wehgetan.* / You have hurt yourself.
> *Er hat **sich** ein Buch gekauft.* / He bought himself a book.
> *Wir nehmen **uns** Geld mit.* / We take money along (for ourselves).
> *Ihr holt **euch** die Zeitung.* / You get the paper (for yourselves).
>
> *Sie machen es **sich** gemütlich.* / They make themselves comfortable.
> *Herr Schmidt, haben Sie **sich** das Taxi bestellt?* / Mr. Schmidt, did you order the cab for yourself?

In German some sentences referring to parts of the body or to clothing use reflexive pronouns.

> EXAMPLES:
>
> *Ich wasche **mir** das Gesicht.* / I wash my face.
> *Ich putze **mir** die Zähne.* / I brush my teeth.
> *Ich kämme **mir** das Haar.* / I comb my hair.
> *Ich ziehe **mir** das Kleid an.* / I put on my dress.
> *Ich setze **mir** die Kappe auf.* / I put on my cap.

The Reflexive Pronouns *einander* and *gegenseitig*

In the sentence *Sie rissen **sich** die Haare aus* (They tore out their hair), it is unclear whether each person tore out his own hair or if each tore out the hair of the other. If the latter is true, the sentence should be changed to:

Sie rissen einander die Haare aus.

OR

Sie rissen sich gegenseitig die Haare aus. / They tore out each other's hair.

Other uses of *einander* (when combined with a preposition) are:

Sie verliebten sich ineinander. / They fell in love with each other.
Sie schämen sich voreinander. / They are ashamed of each other.
Die Männer streiten miteinander. / The men fight with each other.

7.2 POSSESSIVES

Possessives denote ownership. Their use generally corresponds to English usage. Each possessive can be used as an adjective or as an independent pronoun.

The declension of the possessive adjective in the singular follows the pattern of the indefinite article *ein* (see §5.3). The declension of the possessive adjective in the plural follows the pattern of the demonstrative *diese* (see §5.4).

EXAMPLES:

Singular

Indefinite Article	Possessive Adjective
ein Mann / a man	*mein Mann* / my man (husband)
eine Frau / a woman	*meine Frau* / my woman (wife)
ein Kind / a child	*mein Kind* / my child

Plural

Demonstrative
(same for all genders)
diese Kinder / these children   *meine Kinder* / my children

POSSESSIVE ADJECTIVES					
	Singular				
Case	Masc.	Fem.	Neuter	Plural	Meaning
nom.	*mein*	*meine*	*mein*	*meine*	my
acc.	*meinen*	*meine*	*mein*	*meine*	my
dat.	*meinem*	*meiner*	*meinem*	*meinen*	to my
gen.	*meines*	*meiner*	*meines*	*meiner*	of my
nom.	*dein*	*deine*	*dein*	*deine*	your
acc.	*deinen*	*deine*	*dein*	*deine*	your
dat.	*deinem*	*deiner*	*deinem*	*deinen*	to your
gen.	*deines*	*deiner*	*deines*	*deiner*	of your
nom.	*sein*	*seine*	*sein*	*seine*	his
acc.	*seinen*	*seine*	*sein*	*seine*	his
dat.	*seinem*	*seiner*	*seinem*	*seinen*	to his
gen.	*seines*	*seiner*	*seines*	*seiner*	of his
nom.	*ihr*	*ihre*	*ihr*	*ihre*	her
acc.	*ihren*	*ihre*	*ihr*	*ihre*	her
dat.	*ihrem*	*ihrer*	*ihrem*	*ihren*	to her
gen.	*ihres*	*ihrer*	*ihres*	*ihrer*	of her

POSSESSIVE ADJECTIVES					
	Singular				
Case	Masc.	Fem.	Neuter	Plural	Meaning
nom.	*unser*	*uns(e)re*	*unser*	*uns(e)re*	our
acc.	*uns(e)ren*	*uns(e)re*	*unser*	*uns(e)re*	our
dat.	*uns(e)rem*	*uns(e)rer*	*uns(e)rem*	*uns(e)ren*	to our
gen.	*uns(e)res*	*uns(e)rer*	*uns(e)res*	*uns(e)rer*	of our
nom.	*euer*	*eure*	*euer*	*eure*	your
acc.	*euren*	*eure*	*euer*	*eure*	your
dat.	*eurem*	*eurer*	*eurem*	*euren*	to your
gen.	*eures*	*eurer*	*eures*	*eurer*	of your

POSSESSIVE ADJECTIVES

Case	Singular			Plural	Meaning
	Masc.	Fem.	Neuter		
nom.	ihr	ihre	ihr	ihre	their
acc.	ihren	ihre	ihr	ihre	their
dat.	ihrem	ihrer	ihrem	ihren	to their
gen.	ihres	ihrer	ihres	ihrer	of their
nom.	Ihr	Ihre	Ihr	Ihre	your
acc.	Ihren	Ihre	Ihr	Ihre	your
dat.	Ihrem	Ihrer	Ihrem	Ihren	to your
gen.	Ihres	Ihrer	Ihres	Ihrer	of your

The rules for spelling irregularities are as follows: *unser* and *euer* lose the -*e*- of the stem whenever the ending starts with -*e*. However, the full forms can also be used: *unseren, unsere, eueren, euerem,* etc., but never *euerer.*

EXAMPLES:

Meine Schwester ist hübsch. / My sister is pretty.
Ich habe deinen Bleistift. / I have your pencil.
Er hilft seinem Vater. / He helps his father.
Ich mag die Farbe ihres Kleides. / I like the color of her dress.
Sie braucht deine Hilfe. / She needs your help.
Er spricht mit eurer Mutter. / He speaks with your mother.
Hast du unsren Lehrer gesehen? / Did you see our teacher?
Er besucht Ihren Onkel. / He visits your uncle.

A *possessive pronoun* must stand by itself and not precede a noun. If preceded by the definite article, it follows the adjective declension with weak endings (see §6.1 – 1).

EXAMPLES:

Hier ist mein Buch. Wo ist das deine? / Here is my book. Where is yours?
Hat er seinen Kugelschreiber verloren? Gib ihm den meinen. Did he lose his ball-point pen? Give him mine.

- If the possessive pronoun is used without an article, it usually follows the declensional endings of *dieser* (see §5.4

  EXAMPLES:
  *Hier ist ein Mantel. Ist es **deiner?*** / Here is a coat. Is it yours?
  *Hier ist ein Wörterbuch. Ist es **eures?** Ich habe **meines** bei mir.* / Here is a dictionary. Is it yours? I have mine with me.

- If the possessive pronoun is used as a predicate nominativ with the verbs *sein, werden,* or *bleiben,* it takes no ending

  EXAMPLES:
  *Er ist **mein** und bleibt mein.* / He is mine and remains mine.
  *Der Sieg ist **unser.*** / The victory is ours.
  *Der Ring wird morgen **dein**.* / The ring will be yours tomorrow

§7.3 RELATIVE PRONOUNS

A *relative pronoun* introduces a relative clause by referring to a noun or pronoun in the preceding main clause. The element to which the relative pronoun refers is called the *antecedent.*

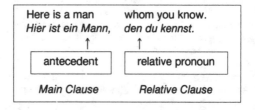

Here is a man	whom you know.
Hier ist ein Mann,	*den du kennst.*
↑	↑
antecedent	relative pronoun
Main Clause	*Relative Clause*

The relative pronouns in German are *der/die/das* (who, that, which), *wer/was* (who, that), and *welcher* (who, that) Their use depends on the context of the sentence.
   The relative pronouns *der/die/das* are declined as follow

	Case	Masc.	Fem.	Neuter	Meaning
S i n g u l a r	*nom.*	*der*	*die*	*das*	that, who, which
	acc.	*den*	*die*	*das*	that, who, which
	dat.	*dem*	*der*	*dem*	to whom, to which
	gen.	*dessen*	*deren*	*dessen*	whose, of which
P l u r a l	*nom.*	*die*			that, who, which
	acc.	*die*	Same for all three genders.		that, who, which
	dat.	*denen*			to whom, to which
	gen.	*deren*			of whom, of which

The gender as well as the number of the relative pronoun
agrees with the gender and the number of its antecedent.
The case of the relative pronoun is determined by its use or
function within the relative clause.

EXAMPLES:

*Kennen Sie den Mann, **der** hier wohnt?* / Do you know the man
who lives here?

*Brauchen Sie das Buch, **das** ich Ihnen lieh?* / Do you need the
book that I lent you?

*Dort sind meine Eltern, bei **denen** ich wohne.* / There are my
parents, with whom I live.

*Das ist das Mädchen, **dessen** Haar ich bewundere.* / That is
the girl whose hair I admire.

The combination of *wo(r)-* with a preposition often replaces
the relative pronoun.

EXAMPLES:
*Hier ist das Haus, **in dem** ich wohne.*

OR

*Hier ist das Haus, **worin** ich wohne.* / Here is the house in
which I live.
*Das ist der Bleistift, **mit dem** ich schreibe.*

OR

*Das ist der Bleistift, **womit** ich schreibe.* / That is the pencil
with which I write.

- *Wo* (where) may be used by itself, instead of a preposition
plus a relative pronoun.

    EXAMPLES:
    *Das ist die Straße, **auf der** wir spielten.* / That is the street on
    which we played.

    OR

    *Das ist die Straße, **wo** wir spielten.* / That is the street where
    we played.

    Note that the relative clause is always separated from
    the main clause by a comma.

- The pronoun *wer* relates to a person or persons who are
not clearly defined.

    EXAMPLE:
    ***Wer** viel studiert, bekommt gute Noten.* / He who studies much
    gets good grades.

- If the antecedent is an indefinite pronoun (see §7.5) or an
adjective used as a neuter noun (*das Netteste* / the nicest),
the relative pronoun **was** can be used.

EXAMPLES:

*Du hast etwas getan, **was** häßlich ist.* / You did something that is ugly.

*Er weiß nichts, **was** wichtig ist.* / He knows nothing that is important.

*Ist das das Netteste, **was** Sie haben?* / Is that the nicest that you have?

The relative pronoun *welcher* takes the same declension as the words *dieser* or *jener* (§5.4). It has no genitive form. Compared with the relative pronouns *der/die/das*, its use is quite limited. It is used primarily for stylistic reasons (such as to avoid repetition).

EXAMPLES:

*Sind Sie die, **welche** heute anfängt?*

> INSTEAD OF

*Sind Sie die, **die** heute anfängt?* / Are you the one who starts today?

*Er sprach mit dem Kind, **welches** das Geld verloren hatte.*

> INSTEAD OF

*Er sprach mit dem Kind, **das** das Geld verloren hatte.* / He spoke to the child who had lost the money.

§7.4 INTERROGATIVE PRONOUNS

An *interrogative pronoun* replaces a noun or noun phrase introducing a question. The main German interrogative pronouns are *wer* (who), *was* (what), and *welcher* (which).

FORMS OF *WER* AND *WAS*			
Case	Masculine and Feminine	Neuter	Meaning
nom.	*wer*	*was*	who, what
acc.	*wen*	*was*	whom, what
dat.	*wem*	—	to whom
gen.	*wessen*	*wessen*	whose

EXAMPLES:
Wer ist da? / Who is here?
Wen sehe ich dort? / Whom do I see there?
Wem soll ich das geben? / To whom shall I give that?
Wessen Schuhe sind das? / Whose shoes are these?
Was ist auf dem Tisch? / What is on the table?
Was tust du? / What are you doing?

Note that there are no separate forms for the masculine and feminine, and there are no plural forms.

- Word combinations with the prefixes *wo-* or *wor-* can be used instead of *was*.

Avoid	Use instead
Mit was schreibst du?	*Womit* schreibst du? / With what are you writing?
Für was ist das gut?	*Wofür* ist das gut? / What is this good for?
An was denkst du?	*Woran* denkst du? / What are you thinking about?
Auf was wartet er?	*Worauf* wartet er? / What is he waiting for?
Von was spricht er?	*Wovon* spricht er? / What is he talking about?

Note: *wo-* combinations cannot be used when referring to people:

Auf wen wartest du? / For whom are you waiting?

The interrogative *welcher* can be used as an adjective or as a pronoun.

FORMS OF *WELCHER*

Case	Masc.	Fem.	Neuter	Meaning
nom.	welcher	welche	welches	which, which one
acc.	welchen	welche	welches	which, which one
dat.	welchem	welcher	welchem	to which, to which one
gen.	welchen	welcher	welchen	of which, of which one
nom.	welche			which, which ones
acc.	welche	Same for all three genders.		which, which ones
dat.	welchen			to which, to which ones
gen.	welcher			of which, of which ones

e form *welches* is used for masculine nouns ending in -*en*
the genitive singular.

EXAMPLE:
Welches Menschen? / of which man?

elcher can be used as an interrogative adjective.

EXAMPLES:
Ruth hat viele Kleider. / Ruth has many dresses.
Welches Kleid hat sie am liebsten? / Which dress does she like
best?
Welche Kleider mag sie nicht? / Which dresses does she not like?

it can be used as an interrogative pronoun.

EXAMPLES:
Ich habe hier drei Platten. / I have here three records.
Welche wollen Sie kaufen? / Which one do you want to buy?
Welche haben Sie schon gehört? / Which one have you heard
already?

- *Kein* is the negative form of the indefinite article *ein*. It indicates the absence of a person or an object. But unlike *ein*, it does have all plural forms, and takes the endings of the definite article *der* (see §5.2).

	Singular			Plural	
Case	Masc.	Fem.	Neuter	All Genders	Meaning
nom.	kein	keine	kein	keine	no, not any, no
acc.	keinen	keine	kein	keine	no, not any, no
dat.	keinem	keiner	keinem	keinen	to none
gen.	keines	keiner	keines	keiner	of none

Kein used as an indefinite adjective:

Er hat keine Zeit. / He has no time.
Das ist in keinem Buch. / That is not in any book.
Er ist ein Mitglied keiner Partei. / He is not a member of any party.

Kein used as an indefinite pronoun:

Keiner von ihnen ist gekommen. / None of them came.
Das tut keiner. / Nobody does that.

§7.5   INDEFINITE PRONOUNS

Indefinite pronouns refer to persons or objects that the speaker cannot or will not identify. A majority of them can also be used as indefinite adjectives.

EXAMPLES:

Indefinite Adjectives	Indefinite Pronouns
alle Bücher / all books	*Alle sind weg.* / All are gone.
ein anderes Mal / another time	*Ein anderer kam.* / Another one came.
einige (mehrere) Leute / some (several) people	*einige (mehrere) blieben.* / Some (several) remained.
jede Frau / each woman	*Jeder hilft.* / Everybody is helping.

IMPORTANT INDEFINITE PRONOUNS			
Stem Indefinite	**For People**	**For Objects**	**Meaning**
all-	alle	alle(s)	all
ander-	andere(r)	andere(s)	other
einig-	einige	einige(s)	some
etwas	—	etwas	something
jed-	jede(r)	jedes	each, every, everybody
jemand	jemand	—	somebody
kein-	keine(r)	keine(s)	no, not any, none, nobody
man	man	—	one, they, people
mehrer-	mehrere	mehrere(s)	several
nichts	—	nichts	nothing
niemand	niemand	—	nobody

The words *etwas* and *nichts* have no declension; *jemand* and *niemand* are seldom declined.

The word *man* always refers to people; it occurs in the nominative only. For the accusative we use *einen,* for the dative, *einer.* There is no plural.

EXAMPLES:
Man spielt heute Hamlet. / Today they play Hamlet.
Er braucht einen nicht. / He does not need one.
Sie gibt einem ein Geschenk. / She gives one a gift.

Verbs

§8.1 WHAT ARE VERBS?

Verbs are words that describe an action, a process, or a state of being. Verbs agree with the person of the subject (first, second, or third person) and with its number (singular or plural).

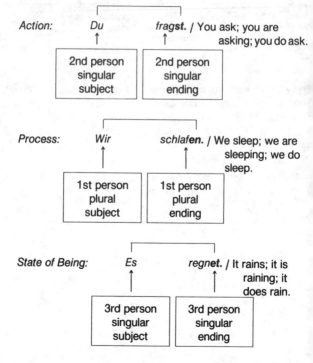

Action: **Du** **fragst.** / You ask; you are asking; you do ask.

2nd person singular subject | 2nd person singular ending

Process: **Wir** **schlafen.** / We sleep; we are sleeping; we do sleep.

1st person plural subject | 1st person plural ending

State of Being: **Es** **regnet.** / It rains; it is raining; it does rain.

3rd person singular subject | 3rd person singular ending

- German verbs are listed in the dictionary in their *infinitive* form. The infinitive ending of a German verb is *-en:*

  *frag**en*** / to ask
  *schlaf**en*** / to sleep
  *regn**en*** / to rain

- The *stems* of these verbs are *frag-,* *schlaf-,* and *regn-.*

  When verbs are conjugated, they change their form to show tense (present tense, past tense, present perfect, etc.), mood (indicative, subjunctive), person, number, and voice (active and passive).

  In German, there are "weak" verbs, which do not change the stem vowel in the past tense and the past participle; "strong" verbs, which do change their stem vowels in these tenses; and irregular verbs, which have features of both weak and strong verbs.

§8.2   THE INDICATIVE MOOD

The *indicative mood* expresses or "indicates" facts. It is used to make statements, exchange information, etc.

§8.2–1   Present Tense

Weak Verbs

The present tense of *weak verbs* is formed as follows:

- Drop the infinitive ending of the verb and add the following endings to the stem:

	Person	Endings	Example	Meaning
S i n g u l a r	1st	-e	*ich frage*	I ask
	2nd	-st (familiar)	*du fragst*	you ask
		-en (formal)	*Sie fragen*	you ask
	3rd *(m.)*	-t	*er fragt*	he asks
	(f.)	-t	*sie fragt*	she asks
	(n.)	-t	*es fragt*	it asks
P l u r a l	1st	-en	*wir fragen*	we ask
	2nd	-t (familiar)	*ihr fragt*	you ask
		-en (formal)	*Sie fragen*	you ask
	3rd	-en	*sie fragen*	they ask

Note: In the conjugation tables that follow, the third person masculine singular will stand also for the feminine and neuter forms: *er (sie, es) fragt* / he (she, it) asks. The second person formal singular is always identical to the second person formal plural. Both of these forms are identical to the third person plural.

- If the stem of the verb ends in *-d, -t, -m,* or *-n,* the vowel *-e* is inserted in the second and third person singular and in the second person plural:

  du findest / you find
  er arbeitet / he works
  ihr atmet / you breathe
  er zeichnet / he draws

  BUT

  er filmt / he films
  du lernst / you learn

f the stem of the verb ends in -*s*, -*ß*, -*x*, or -*z*, the -*s*- in the
ending of the second person singular is omitted:

du rast / you speed
du haßt / you hate
du mixt / you mix
du setzt / you put

f the stem of the verb ends in -*eln*, the -*e*- is dropped in the
first person singular, as in the verbs *klingeln* (to ring),
lächeln (to smile), and *sammeln* (to collect):

ich klingle / I ring
ich lächle / I smile
ich sammle / I collect

f the stem of the verb ends in -*eln* or -*ern*, the ending for
the first and third person plural is -*n;* they have the same
form as the infinitive:

wir lächeln / we smile
sie ändern / they change

Examples of Weak Verbs in the Present Tense

Er findet das Buch. / He finds the book.
Arbeitest du schwer? / Do you work hard?
Zeichnest du einen Baum? / Do you draw a tree?
Du rast doch wie ein Verrückter! / You speed like a madman.
Warum setzt du dich nicht? / Why don't you sit down?
Ich sammle Briefmarken. / I collect postage stamps.
Wir lächeln darüber. / We smile about it.

Strong Verbs

n the present tense, *strong verbs* change their stem vowels
as follows:
Strong verbs with the stem vowel -*a*- change it to -*ä*- in the
second and third person singular:

ich fahre / I drive	*ich schlafe* / I sleep
du fährst / you drive	*du schläfst* / you sleep
er fährt / he drives	*er schläft* / he sleeps

- Those with the stem vowel *-e-* change it to *-i-* or *-ie-*:

ich gebe / I give	*ich lese* / I read
du gibst / you give	*du liest* / you read
er gibt / he gives	*er liest* / he reads

Note the following changes in spelling:

ich esse / I eat	*ich nehme* / I take
du ißt / you eat	*du nimmst* / you take
er ißt / he eats	*er nimmt* / he takes

- The verbs *gehen* (to go) and *stehen* (to stand) have an *-e-* vowel in the stem, but they *do not* change it:

ich gehe / I go	*ich stehe* / I stand
du gehst / you go	*du stehst* / you stand
er geht / he goes	*er steht* / he stands

- The verbs *wissen* (to know) and *tun* (to do) are irregular in the singular and plural:

ich weiß / I know	*ich tu(e)* / I do
du weißt / you know	*du tust* / you do
er weiß / he knows	*er tut* / he does
wir wissen / we know	*wir tun* / we do
ihr wißt / you know	*ihr tut* / you do
sie wissen / they know	*sie tun* / they do

Examples of Strong Verbs in the Present Tense

Schläfst du, wenn du fährst? / Do you sleep when you drive?
Er gibt ihm Geld. / He gives him money.
Sie ißt ihr Frühstück. / She eats her breakfast.
Du nimmst die Zeitung. / You take the paper.
Gehst du ins Kino? / Do you go to the movies?
Wo steht er? / Where is he standing?
Weißt du das nicht? / Don't you know that?
Wir tun das nicht. / We don't do that.

Continued Action

When expressing a situation that started in the past and continues into the present, we use the present perfect in English and the present tense in German.

> EXAMPLES:
> *Ich arbeite schon drei Jahre für diese Firma.* / I have been working for this firm for three years.
>
> *Ich bin schon seit zwei Tagen hier.* / I have been here for two days.
>
> Note: The time phrase is usually accompanied by *schon* (already), *seit* (since), or by *schon seit* — telltale signs of continued action.

Auxiliary Verbs

There are three auxiliary (or helping) verbs in German: the verbs *sein* (to be), *haben* (to have), and *werden* (to become, get, grow, come to be). The verbs *sein* and *haben* are as commonly used in German as are their equivalents in English. They can be used as words in their own right, but usually they help to form other verb forms. All three verbs are irregular.

sein / to be	
ich bin / I am	*wir sind* / we are
du bist / you are	*ihr seid* / you are
er ist / he is	*sie sind* / they are

EXAMPLES:
Ich bin Lehrer. / I am a teacher.
Bist du zu Hause? / Are you at home?
Wir sind zufrieden. / We are satisfied.

> *haben* / to have
> *ich habe* / I have   *wir haben* / we have
> *du hast* / you have   *ihr habt* / you have
> *er hat* / he has   *sie haben* / they have

EXAMPLES:

Du hast ein Auto. / You have a car.
Sie hat ein hübsches Kleid. / She has a pretty dress.
Haben Sie einen Computer? / Do you have a computer?

> *werden* / to become, get, grow, come to be
> *ich werde* / I become   *wir werden* / we become
> *du wirst* / you become   *ihr werdet* / you become
> *er wird* / he becomes   *sie werden* / they become

EXAMPLES:

Er wird Arzt. / He becomes (is becoming) a doctor.
Wirst du böse? / Do you get angry?
Wir werden reich. / We come to be (are getting) rich.

§8.2–2 Past Tense

The *past tense,* also called *imperfect,* is used in German primarily to report or narrate past events, sometimes a recurring or habitual action—especially in written or formal usage.

EXAMPLES:

Voriges Jahr wohnte er in München. / Last year he lived in Munich.
Um sechs Uhr machte er gewöhnlich einen Spaziergang. / At six o'clock he usually went for a walk.

Weak Verbs

The past tense of *weak verbs* is formed by adding the following endings to the verb stem:

	Person	Ending	Example	Meaning
S i n g u l a r	1st	*-te*	*ich fragte*	I asked
	2nd	*-test*	*du fragtest*	you asked
	3rd	*-te*	*er fragte*	he asked
P l u r a l	1st	*-ten*	*wir fragten*	we asked
	2nd	*-tet*	*ihr fragtet*	you asked
	3rd	*-ten*	*sie fragten*	they asked

If the stem of the verb ends in *-d, -t, -m,* or *-n,* the vowel *-e-* is inserted between the stem and the ending.

EXAMPLES:
es blendete / it blinded
du arbeitetest / you worked
wir atmeten / we breathed
sie zeichnete / she drew

BUT

er filmte / he filmed
er lernte / he learned

Strong Verbs

To form the past tense, *strong verbs* change their stem vowels and take the following endings:

nehmen / to take	*fangen* / to catch	*fahren* / to drive
ich nahm / I took	*ich fing* / I caught	*ich fuhr* / I drove
du nahmst / you took	*du fingst* / you caught	*du fuhrst* / you drove
er nahm / he took	*er fing* / he caught	*er fuhr* / he drove
wir nahmen / we took	*wir fingen* / we caught	*wir fuhren* / we drove
ihr nahmt / you took	*ihr fingt* / you caught	*ihr fuhrt* / you drove
sie nahmen / they took	*sie fingen* / they caught	*sie fuhren* / they drove

EXAMPLES:
Wir nahmen Theaterkarten für morgen. / We took theater
   tickets for tomorrow.
Fingst du den Ball, Peter? / Did you catch the ball, Peter?
Gestern nahm ich das Auto und fuhr nach Rom. / Yesterday I
   took the car and drove to Rome.

Note: For an extensive treatment of strong verbs, see
§8.2–3.

Irregular Verbs

Irregular verbs change the vowel in the stem and, in addi-
tion, take weak verb endings.

Infinitive	Meaning	Past Tense (3rd Person)	Meaning
brennen	to burn	*es brannte*	it burned
kennen	to know	*er kannte*	he knew
nennen	to name	*er nannte*	he named
rennen	to run	*er rannte*	he ran
senden	to send	*er sandte*	he sent
wenden	to turn	*er wandte*	he turned
bringen	to bring	*er brachte*	he brought
denken	to think	*er dachte*	he thought
wissen	to know	*er wußte*	he knew

EXAMPLES:

Kanntest du diesen Mann? / Did you know this man?
Das Kind rannte nach dem Ball. / The child ran after the ball.
Er brachte mir ein Buch. / He brought me a book.
Dachten Sie an Ihre Mutter? / Did you think of your mother?
Ich wußte das nicht. / I did not know that.

Auxiliary Verbs

sein / to be	
ich war / I was	*wir waren* / we were
du warst / you were	*ihr wart* / you were
er war / he was	*sie waren* / they were
haben / to have	
ich hatte / I had	*wir hatten* / we had
du hattest / you had	*ihr hattet* / you had
er hatte / he had	*sie hatten* / they had
werden / to become	
ich wurde / I became	*wir wurden* / we became
du wurdest / you became	*ihr wurdet* / you became
er wurde / he became	*sie wurden* / they became

EXAMPLES:

Warst du gestern im Kino? / Were you at the movies yesterday?
Wart ihr in der Schule? / Were you in school?
Er hatte eine Erkältung. / He had a cold.
Er wurde Arzt. / He became a doctor.

§8.2–3 Present Perfect Tense

Weak Verbs

The *present perfect tense* is the verb form used most frequently in German, next to the present tense. It is the tense commonly used in conversation and is, in most instances, the equivalent of the English past tense.

- The present perfect is formed by taking the present tense of the auxiliary verbs *haben* or *sein* plus the past participle of the main verb.

- Most of the German past participles are formed with *ge-* preceding the stem of the verb. If the verb is weak, the ending is *-t* or *-et*. If strong, the ending is *-en* (see the following section).

EXAMPLE:

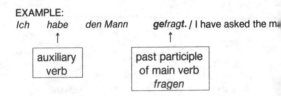

Ich   habe   den Mann   gefragt. / I have asked the ma

auxiliary verb

past participle of main verb *fragen*

Note: The present participle always stands at the end o the clause.

EXAMPLES:
Hast du Deutsch gelernt? / Did you learn German?
Wir haben ihn gefragt. / We asked him.
Sie hat viel gearbeitet. / She worked a great deal.

- Weak Verbs ending in *-ieren* do not take the prefix *ge-* in the formation of the past participle.

EXAMPLES:
buchstabieren / to spell
Er hat mir das Wort buchstabiert. / He spelled the word for r
reparieren / to repair
Haben Sie die Schuhe repariert? / Did you repair the shoes?
studieren / to study
Sie hat den ganzen Tag studiert. / She studied all day.

Auxiliary Verbs

sein / to be	
ich bin gewesen / I have been	*wir sind gewesen* / we have been
du bist gewesen / you have been	*ihr seid gewesen* / you have been
er ist gewesen / he has been	*sie sind gewesen* / they have been
haben / to have	
ich habe gehabt / I have had	*wir haben gehabt* / we have had
du hast gehabt / you have had	*ihr habt gehabt* / you have had
er hat gehabt / he has had	*sie haben gehabt* / they have had
werden / to become	
ich bin geworden / I have become	*wir sind geworden* / we have become
du bist geworden / you have become	*ihr seid geworden* / you have become
er ist geworden / he has become	*sie sind geworden* / they have become

EXAMPLES:

Wir sind heute zu Hause gewesen. / We have been (were) at home today.

Ist er im Konzert gewesen? / Has he been (Was he) at the concert?

Hast du die Prüfung gehabt? / Did you have (Have you had) the exam?

Ist dein Bruder Rechtsanwalt geworden? / Did your brother (Has your brother) become a lawyer?

Strong Verbs

There are groups of strong verbs that change the stem
vowel of the infinitive to form the past tense and the past
participle. As with English irregular verbs, the vowel
changes of the German strong verbs have to be memoriz

- In the table below, the infinitive, past tense, and past
  participle each have a different stem vowel.

Infinitive	Past Tense (3rd person)	Past Participle	Meaning
1. STEM VOWELS _E-A-O_			
befehlen	befahl	befohlen	to order
brechen	brach	gebrochen	to break
empfehlen	empfahl	empfohlen	to recommen
nehmen	nahm	genommen	to take
sprechen	sprach	gesprochen	to speak
stehlen	stahl	gestohlen	to steal
sterben	starb	gestorben	to die
treffen	traf	getroffen	to meet
werben	warb	geworben	to advertise
2. STEM VOWELS _I-A-E_			
bitten	bat	gebeten	to ask
liegen	lag	gelegen	to lie
sitzen	saß	gesessen	to sit

Infinitive	Past Tense (3rd person)	Past Participle	Meaning
3. STEM VOWELS *I-A-O*			
beginnen	*begann*	*begonnen*	to begin
gewinnen	*gewann*	*gewonnen*	to win
schwimmen	*schwamm*	*geschwommen*	to swim
4. STEM VOWELS *I-A-U*			
binden	*band*	*gebunden*	to bind
gelingen	*gelang*	*gelungen*	to succeed
klingen	*klang*	*geklungen*	to sound
schwingen	*schwang*	*geschwungen*	to swing
singen	*sang*	*gesungen*	to sing
springen	*sprang*	*gesprungen*	to spring
trinken	*trank*	*getrunken*	to drink
zwingen	*zwang*	*gezwungen*	to force

In the table below, the past participle has the same stem vowel as the infinitive.

Infinitive	Past Tense (3rd Person)	Past Participle	Meaning
1. STEM VOWELS *A-I(IE)-A*			
fangen	*fing*	*gefangen*	to catch
blasen	*blies*	*geblasen*	to blow
braten	*briet*	*gebraten*	to broil

Infinitive	Past Tense (3rd Person)	Past Participle	Meaning
fallen	*fiel*	*gefallen*	to fall
raten	*riet*	*geraten*	to advise
schlafen	*schlief*	*geschlafen*	to sleep
2. STEM VOWELS *A-U-A*			
backen	*buk, backte*	*gebacken*	to bake
fahren	*fuhr*	*gefahren*	to drive
graben	*grub*	*gegraben*	to dig
laden	*lud*	*geladen*	to load
schlagen	*schlug*	*geschlagen*	to beat
tragen	*trug*	*getragen*	to carry
waschen	*wusch*	*gewaschen*	to wash
3. STEM VOWELS *AU-IE-AU*			
laufen	*lief*	*gelaufen*	to run
4. STEM VOWELS *E-A-E*			
essen	*aß*	*gegessen*	to eat
geschehen	*geschah*	*geschehen*	to happen
sehen	*sah*	*gesehen*	to see
lesen	*las*	*gelesen*	to read
messen	*maß*	*gemessen*	to measure
sehen	*sah*	*gesehen*	to see
treten	*trat*	*getreten*	to step

Infinitive	Past Tense (3rd person)	Past Participle	Meaning
5. STEM VOWELS *EI-IE-EI*			
heißen	hieß	geheißen	to be called
6. STEM VOWELS *O-A-O*			
kommen	kam	gekommen	to come
7. STEM VOWELS *O-IE-O*			
stoßen	stieß	gestoßen	to push
8. STEM VOWELS *U-IE-U*			
rufen	rief	gerufen	to call

n the table below, the past participle has the same stem
owel as the past tense.

Infinitive	Past Tense (3rd person)	Past Participle	Meaning
1. STEM VOWELS *E-A-A*			
stehen	stand	gestanden	to stand
2. STEM VOWELS *E-O-O*			
heben	hob	gehoben	to lift
schwellen	schwoll	geschwollen	to swell

Infinitive	Past Tense (3rd Person)	Past Participle	Meaning
3. STEM VOWELS EI-I(IE)-I(IE)			
beißen	*biß*	*gebissen*	to bite
gleichen	*glich*	*geglichen*	to resemble
reiten	*ritt*	*geritten*	to ride
bleiben	*blieb*	*geblieben*	to remain
preisen	*pries*	*gepriesen*	to praise
schneiden	*schnitt*	*geschnitten*	to cut
4. STEM VOWELS IE-O-O			
bieten	*bot*	*geboten*	to offer
fliegen	*flog*	*geflogen*	to fly
fließen	*floß*	*geflossen*	to flow
frieren	*fror*	*gefroren*	to freeze
ziehen	*zog*	*gezogen*	to draw
5. STEM VOWELS Ö-O-O			
schwören	*schwor*	*geschworen*	to swear
6. STEM VOWELS Ü-O-O			
lügen	*log*	*gelogen*	to lie

- In the examples below, the first German sentence uses the past tense of the verb, and the second sentence uses the present perfect.

EXAMPLES:

Er sprach mit ihr. Er hat mit ihr gesprochen. / He talked with her.

Traf er ihn? Hat er ihn getroffen? / Did he meet him?

Sie bat ihn um Geld. Sie hat ihn um Geld gebeten. / She asked him for money.

Gestern begannen wir damit. Gestern haben wir damit begonnen. / Yesterday we started with it.

Sie sang das Lied. Sie hat das Lied gesungen. / She sang the song.

Wir tranken Wein. Wir haben Wein getrunken. / We drank wine.

Das Kind schlief gut. Das Kind hat gut geschlafen. / The child slept well.

Wir aßen Frühstück. Wir haben Frühstück gegessen. / We ate breakfast.

Er trug einen Hut. Er hat einen Hut getragen. / He wore a hat.

Sie wusch sich. Sie hat sich gewaschen. / She washed herself.

Du lasest die Zeitung. Du hast die Zeitung gelesen. / You read the paper.

Sahst du sie nicht? Hast du sie nicht gesehen? / Did you not see her?

Transitive and Intransitive Verbs

A *transitive verb* is capable of taking a direct object in the accusative:

Er hat das Buch gekauft. / He bought the book.

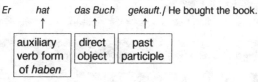

An *intransitive verb* is incapable of taking a direct object:

Sie ist gekommen. / She came.

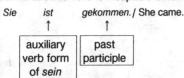

Die Bäume   *sind*   *gewachsen.* / The trees grew.

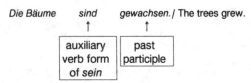

Many German verbs use the auxiliary verb *sein* (instead of *haben*) to form the present perfect *provided that* the main verb is intransitive and that it indicates a change of location or of condition.

- The following is a list of the more common German verbs that take *sein* as their auxiliary because they denote a change of location:

fahren / to travel	*klettern* / to climb
fallen / to fall	*kommen* / to come
fliegen / to fly	*schwimmen* / to swim
gehen / to go	

- These verbs take *sein* because they indicate a change in condition:

aufwachen / to wake up	*sterben* / to die
einschlafen / to fall asleep	*wachsen* / to grow
ertrinken / to drown	

- These verbs also take *sein* as their auxiliary:

begegnen / to meet	*gelingen* / to succeed
bleiben / to remain	*mißglücken* / to fail

Examples of Intransitive Verbs in the Present Perfect

Er ist ins Theater gegangen. / He went to the theater.
Wir sind nach Wien geflogen. / We flew to Vienna.
Sie ist verschwunden. / She disappeared.
Er ist ertrunken. / He drowned.
Ist sie gestorben? / Did she die?
Wir sind zu Hause geblieben. / We stayed at home.
Es ist ihm gelungen. / He succeeded.

Irregular Verbs (see Sec. 8.2-2)

Infinitive	Meaning	Past Tense (3rd Person)	Past Participle	Meaning
brennen	to burn	*brannte*	*gebrannt*	burned
kennen	to know	*kannte*	*gekannt*	knew
nennen	to name	*nannte*	*genannt*	named
rennen	to run	*rannte*	*gerannt*	ran
senden	to send	*sandte*	*gesandt*	sent
wenden	to turn	*wandte*	*gewandt*	turned
bringen	to bring	*brachte*	*gebracht*	brought
denken	to think	*dachte*	*gedacht*	thought
wissen	to know	*wußte*	*gewußt*	knew

Note: The forms *sendete, gesendet* (sent), and *wendete, gewendet* (turned) are also used.

EXAMPLES:
Das Haus hat gebrannt. / The house burned.
Er hat mir ein Buch gesandt. / He sent me a book.
Hast du dich an sie gewandt? / Did you turn to her?
Ich habe nicht daran gedacht. / I did not think of it.

§8.2-4 Past Perfect Tense

The *past perfect* (or pluperfect) consists of the past tense of the auxiliary verbs *haben* or *sein* plus the past participle of the main verb. This tense indicates a past event that took place *before* another past event.

EXAMPLES:
Er war müde, weil er schlecht geschlafen hatte. / He was tired because he had slept badly.

↑ past tense

↑ past perfect tense

Eva war traurig, weil ihr Freund sie nicht besucht hatte. / Eva was sad because her friend had not visited her.

Er war zornig, weil sie nicht gekommen war. / He was angry because she had not come.

Auxiliary Verbs

sein / to be	
ich war gewesen / I had been	*wir waren gewesen* / we had been
du warst gewesen / you had been	*ihr wart gewesen* / you had been
er war gewesen / he had been	*sie waren gewesen* / they had been
haben / to have	
ich hatte gehabt / I had had	*wir hatten gehabt* / we had had
du hattest gehabt / you had had	*ihr hattet gehabt* / you had had
er hatte gehabt / he had had	*sie hatten gehabt* / they had had
werden / to become	
ich war geworden / I had become	*wir waren geworden* / we had become
du warst geworden / you had become	*ihr wart geworden* / you had become
er war geworden / he had become	*sie waren geworden* / they had become

EXAMPLES:

Ich war zu Hause gewesen, als du kamst. / I had been at home when you came.

Ich hatte Durst gehabt, bevor ich etwas bestellte. / I had been thirsty before I ordered something.

Sie war Krankenpflegerin geworden, bevor sie Ärztin wurde. / She had been a nurse before she became a doctor.

§8.2–5 Future Tense

The *future* tense is formed from the present tense of the auxiliary verb *werden* plus the infinitive of the main verb. In German, the infinitive always stands at the end of the sentence.

EXAMPLES:
Ich werde nach New York fahren. / I will drive to New York.
Wirst du das Buch kaufen? / Will you buy the book?
Wir werden spät aufstehen. / We will get up late.

- Wherever a time phrase (e.g., *nächstes Jahr* / next year, *morgen* / tomorrow) implies that something will happen in the future, the future tense can be replaced by the present tense:

  Nächstes Jahr fahre ich nach Kanada. / Next year I'll go to Canada.
  Morgen bleibe ich zu Hause. / Tomorrow I'll stay at home.

- In certain phrases the present is preferred to the future tense:

  Er kommt nie her. / He will never come here.
  Ich bin gleich dort. / I'll be there right away.
  Ich seh dich um 8 Uhr. / I'll see you at 8 o'clock.

- Sometimes the future tense is used to express probability or likelihood:

  Wo ist Otto? / Where is Otto?
  Er wird in der Schule sein. / He is probably at school.
  Ich habe den neuen Mercedes gesehen, aber der wird zu teuer sein. / I have seen the new Mercedes, but it is probably too expensive.

Auxiliary Verbs

sein / to be	
ich werde sein / I will be	*wir werden sein* / we will be
du wirst sein / you will be	*ihr werdet sein* / you will be
er wird sein / he will be	*sie werden sein* / they will be

haben / to have	
ich werde haben / I will have	*wir werden haben* / we will have
du wirst haben / you will have	*ihr werdet haben* / you will have
er wird haben / he will have	*sie werden haben* / they will have

werden / to become	
ich werde werden / I will become	*wir werden werden* / we will become
du wirst werden / you will become	*ihr werdet werden* / you will become
er wird werden / he will become	*sie werden werden* / they will become

EXAMPLES:

Wenn ich komme, wird auch er dort sein. / When I come, he will be there too.

Werden Sie es haben, wenn ich es brauche? / Will you have it when I need it?

Wird er der nächste Präsident werden? / Will he become the next president?

§8.2–6 Future Perfect Tense

The *future perfect tense* is formed from the present tense of *werden*, the past participle of the main verb, and the auxiliary verbs *haben* or *sein* at the end of the sentence. This tense is used rarely.

EXAMPLES:
Er wird lange gearbeitet haben. / He will have worked long.
Sie wird sehr müde gewesen sein. / She will have been very tired.

§8.3 THE IMPERATIVE

The *imperative* is used to express requests or commands. In German, an exclamation point is used after a command most of the time. The imperative is used only in the present tense.

- The familiar command in the singular is formed by removing the *-st* or *-t* ending from the second person singular.

EXAMPLES:
Du sagst / You say. *Sag!* / Say!
Du gehst / You go. *Geh!* / Go!
Du trinkst / You drink. *Trink!* / Drink!
Du gibst / You give. *Gib!* / Give!
Du liest / You read. *Lies!* / Read!
Du ißt / You eat. *Iß!* / Eat!

- Verbs that use the umlaut in the second person singular *do not* change the stem vowel in the familiar imperative:

EXAMPLES:
Du wäschst dich. / You wash yourself. *Wasch dich!* / Wash yourself.
Du fällst nicht. / You don't fall. *Fall nicht!* / Don't fall.

- An *e* should be added to the stem of the verb if the verb ends in *-d*, *-t*, *-m*, *-n*, or *-ig*:

EXAMPLES:

Wende dich um! / Turn around.
Arbeite mehr! / Work more.
Atme tief! / Breathe deeply.
Rechne mir das aus! / Figure that out for me.
Entschuldige, bitte! / Excuse me, please.

- If the infinitive of the verb ends in *-eln,* the *-e-* is eliminated, but an *-e* ending is added:

  EXAMPLES:

Infinitive	Imperative
lächeln / to smile	*Lächle!* / Smile!
behandeln / to treat	*Behandle (ihn)!* / Treat (him).

- The familiar command in the plural is formed by using the second person plural without the *ihr:*

  EXAMPLES:

  Kommt nach Hause! / Come home (you two).
  Holt die Zeitung! / Get the paper (boys).
  Kauft nicht zu viel! / Don't buy too much (folks).

- The formal command has the same form for both singular and plural; it is formed by the infinitive followed by *Sie:*

  EXAMPLES:

  Kommen Sie her! / Come here.
  Nehmen Sie Platz! / Take a seat.
  Parken Sie den Wagen! / Park the car.

- The equivalent of the English "let's. . ." is formed by using the first person plural of the verb, followed by *wir:*

  EXAMPLES:

  Gehen wir nach Hause! / Let's go home.
  Besuchen wir ihn! / Let's visit him.
  Studieren wir jetzt! / Let's study now.

- The equivalent of the English "Be so good . . ." is formed by using *sei* for the singular familiar, *seid* for the plural familiar, and *seien Sie* for the plural formal:

EXAMPLES:

Sei so gut und hilf mir damit. / Be so good as to help me with it.
Seid so gut und helft uns. / Be so good as to help us.
Seien Sie so gut und helfen Sie uns. / Be so good as to help us.

The infinitive as command form is used with impersonal instructions and, sometimes, with commands meant to be harsh:

EXAMPLES:

Links fahren. / Drive left.
Einsteigen. / All aboard!
Auf die Bremse steigen. / Step on the brakes.
Mund (Maul) halten. / Shut up!

Note: an exclamation point after commands of this kind is unnecessary.

Negative commands are formed in the same manner as positive commands. In German there is no construction exactly matching the English *Do not. . . .* or *Don't. . . .*

EXAMPLES:

Sprich nicht so schnell!! / Don't talk so fast.
Trinkt nicht so viel Kaffee! / Don't drink so much coffee.
Rauchen Sie nicht! / Don't smoke.
Bitte nicht stören / Please do not disturb.

§8.4 THE SUBJUNCTIVE MOOD

The *subjunctive mood* expresses a point of view, doubt, fear, hope—in short, anything that is not a fact. It can be considered as a counterpart to the indicative mood.

Auxiliary Verbs

The auxiliary verbs *sein* and *haben* in the subjunctive are as follows:

SEIN / TO BE

Past Tense Indicative	Present Tense Subjunctive
ich war / I was	*ich wäre* / I would be
du warst / you were	*du wärest* / you would be
er war / he was	*er wäre* / he would be
wir waren / we were	*wir wären* / we would be
ihr wart / you were	*ihr wäret* / you would be
sie waren / they were	*sie wären* / they would be

Past Tense Subjunctive

ich wäre gewesen / I would have been
du wärest gewesen / you would have been
er wäre gewesen / he would have been
wir wären gewesen / we would have been
ihr wäret gewesen / you would have been
sie wären gewesen / they would have been

HABEN / TO HAVE

Past Tense Indicative	Present Tense Subjunctive
ich hatte / I had	*ich hätte* / I would have
du hattest / you had	*du hättest* / you would have
er hatte / he had	*er hätte* / he would have
wir hatten / we had	*wir hätten* / we would have
ihr hattet / you had	*ihr hättet* / you would have
sie hatten / they had	*sie hätten* / they would have

Past Tense Subjunctive

ich hätte gehabt / I would have had
du hättest gehabt / you would have had
er hätte gehabt / he would have had
wir hätten gehabt / we would have had
ihr hättet gehabt / you would have had
sie hätten gehabt / they would have had

EXAMPLES:

Wäre ich nur jünger!

OR

Wenn ich nur jünger wäre! / If only I were younger!

Wärest du nur hier gewesen! OR

Wenn du nur hier gewesen wärest! / If only you had been here!

Hätte er nur mehr Geduld! OR

Wenn er nur mehr Geduld hätte! / If only he had more patience!

Hätten wir nur mehr Geld gehabt!

OR

Wenn wir nur mehr Geld gehabt hätten! / If only we had had
more money!

Here are some other verbs used with *wäre* and *hätte*:

Wärest du nur gekommen! / If only you had come!
Hätten Sie es nur getan! / If only you had done it!

Weak Verbs

The present tense of the subjunctive for weak verbs is
identical to the past tense indicative.

ich glaubte / I believed	*wir glaubten* / we believed
du glaubtest / you believed	*ihr glaubtet* / you believed
er glaubte / he believed	*sie glaubten* / they believed

EXAMPLE:
Glaubte er mir nur!

OR

Wenn er mir nur glaubte! / If he would only believe me!

For clarity's sake, particularly in the spoken and colloquial
use of the language, the form *würde* (would) is used to
express weak verbs (and many strong ones) in the subjunctive.

Forms of *würde*	
ich würde / I would	*wir würden* / we would
du würdest / you would	*ihr würdet* / you would
er würde / he would	*sie würden* / they would

EXAMPLES:

Würde er mir nur glauben! / If only he would believe me!
Würdest du das Haus kaufen? / Would you buy the house?
Sie weiß, daß ich es sagen würde. / She knows that I would say it.
Sie weiß, daß ich es gesagt haben würde. / She knows that I would have said it.

Strong and Irregular Verbs

Strong and irregular verbs are formed by adding the subjunctive endings *-e*, *-est*, *-e*, *-en*, *-et*, and *-en* to the stem of the verb in the past tense. Verbs containing the vowels *a*, *o*, or *u* in the stem add an umlaut.

Infinitive	Past Tense	Present Tense Subjunctive
schlafen / to sleep	*ich schlief* / I slept	*ich schliefe* / I would sleep
geben / to give	*du gabst* / you gave	*du gäbest* / you would give
fliegen / to fly	*er flog* / he flew	*er flöge* / he would fly
schlagen / to beat	*wir schlugen* / we beat	*wir schlügen* / we would beat
bringen / to bring	*ihr brachtet* / you brought	*ihr brächtet* / you would bring
wissen / to know	*sie wußten* / they knew	*sie wüßten* / they would know

EXAMPLES:

Mit einer Million in der Bank, schliefe ich besser, schlüge mir die Sorgen aus dem Kopf, und flöge morgen nach Tahiti. / With a million in the bank, I would sleep better, forget my troubles and fly to Tahiti tomorrow.

Er brächte dir gern Blumen./ He would like to bring you flowers.
Wüßten wir doch die Antwort!/ If only we knew the answer.

Some strong and irregular verbs in the subjunctive, present
and past tense, 1st person singular, are shown in the table.

Infinitive	Past Tense Indicative	Present Tense Subjunctive	Past Tense Subjunctive
bleiben	*ich blieb /* I stayed	*ich bliebe /* I would stay	*ich wäre geblieben /* I would have stayed
bringen	*ich brachte /* I brought	*ich brächte /* I would bring	*ich hätte gebracht /* I would have brought
denken	*ich dachte /* I thought	*ich dächte /* I would think	*ich hätte gedacht /* I would have thought
finden	*ich fand /* I found	*ich fände /* I would find	*ich hätte gefunden /* I would have found
gehen	*ich ging /* I went	*ich ginge /* I would go	*ich wäre gegangen /* I would have gone
halten	*ich hielt /* I held	*ich hielte /* I would hold	*ich hätte gehalten /* I would have held
kommen	*ich kam /* I came	*ich käme /* I would come	*ich wäre gekommen /* I would have come
wissen	*ich wußte /* I knew	*ich wüßte /* I would know	*ich hätte gewußt /* I would have known

EXAMPLES:

Present Tense Subjunctive

Ich wollte, er bliebe zu Hause.

OR

Ich wollte, er würde zu Hause bleiben. / I wished he would stay
home.

Past Tense Subjunctive

Ich wollte, er wäre zu Hause geblieben. / I wished he would
have stayed home.

Present Tense Subjunctive

Ich wünschte, er fände den Ring.

OR

Ich wünschte, er würde den Ring finden. / I wished he would
find the ring.

Past Tense Subjunctive
Ich wünschte, er hätte den Ring gefunden. / I wished he would have found the ring.

Present Tense Subjunctive
Ich wollte, er wüßte die Adresse.

OR

Ich wollte, er würde die Adresse wissen. / I wished he would know the address.

Past Tense Subjunctive
Ich wollte, er hätte die Adresse gewußt. / I wished he would have known the address.

§8.5 THE CONDITIONAL MOOD

The *conditional mood* is the grammatical form usually introduced by *wenn* (if). It expresses a condition: "I would do it, if . . . ." It is used in the same way as the English conditional.

• The indicative mood must be used in both parts of a conditional sentence if nothing in the clause introduced by *wenn* is contrary to fact.

EXAMPLES:
Wenn ich Zeit habe, lese ich ein Buch.

OR

Ich lese ein Buch, wenn ich Zeit habe.

OR

Habe ich Zeit, so lese ich ein Buch. / If I have time, I will read a book.

Note: in the last version the *wenn* is implied.

• Present contrary-to-fact situations are expressed by the present tense of the subjunctive.

EXAMPLES:
Wenn ich Zeit hätte, würde ich ein Buch lesen. / If I had time, I would read a book.

Wenn es nicht schneite, würde ich früher kommen.

OR

Wenn es nicht schneite, käme ich früher. / If it did not snow, I would come earlier.

- Past contrary-to-fact situations can be expressed by the past tense of the subjunctive or by the *würde* construction:

    Subjunctive:
    Wenn es nicht geschneit hätte, wäre ich früher nach Hause gekommen.
    Würde Construction:
    Wenn es nicht geschneit hätte, würde ich früher nach Hause gekommen sein. / If it had not snowed, I would have come home earlier.

- Some of the umlauted subjunctive verbs are often replaced by the *würde* construction: *ich brächte, ich würde bringen* (I would bring); *ich dächte, ich würde denken* (I would think); *ich fände, ich würde finden* (I would find); *ich käme, ich würde kommen* (I would come).

- Sometimes the *würde* in a *wenn* clause can be substituted for a modal verb (see §8.8), although the meaning of the sentence might change slightly.

    Wenn du es mir bringen solltest (instead of *bringen würdest* or *brächtest*), *würde ich mich sehr freuen.* / If you would bring it to me, I would be very happy.

    Wenn er mir helfen wollte (instead of *hülfe* or *helfen würde*), *könnte ich studieren.* / If he would (wanted to) help me, I could study.

    Wenn ich mit ihm sprechen könnte (instead of *spräche* or *sprechen würde*), *wäre die Sache in Ordnung.* / If I could talk to him, the situation would be all right.

- Constructions introduced by *als ob* (as if):

> *Er schreit, als ob er verrückt wäre.* / He shouts as if he were crazy
> *Es sieht aus, als ob es morgen schneien würde.* / It looks as if it
>   would snow tomorrow.
> *Er tut, als ob er das nicht gewußt hätte.* / He acts as if he had
>   not known that.

§8.6 MISCELLANEOUS CATEGORIES

§8.6–1 Impersonal Verbs

Impersonal verbs, introduced by the pronoun *es* (it), are as
common in German as they are in English.

- Impersonal verbs referring to natural phenomena are used
the same way in both languages.

EXAMPLES:

Es ist warm. / It is warm.	*Es friert.* / It is freezing.
Es ist kalt. / It is cold.	*Es tagt.* / It dawns
Es regnet. / It rains	(is dawning).
(is raining).	*Es dämmert.* / It darkens
Es schneit. / It snows	(is getting dark).
(is snowing).	*Es ist schwül.* / It is muggy.

- Here are some expressions that take the pronoun *es* in
German and the pronoun *I* in English.

> *Es enttäuscht mich, daß . . .* / I am disappointed (it
>   disappoints me) that . . .
> *Es erstaunt mich, daß . . .* / I am amazed (it amazes me)
>   that . . .
> *Es freut mich, daß . . .* / I am glad (it gladdens me) that . . .
> *Es gefällt mir hier.* / I like it here.
> *Es tut mir leid.* / I am sorry.
> *Es ist mir recht.* / I agree to it.

- Here are some examples using the expression *es gibt*
(there is, there are)

> *Es gibt heute Wiener Schnitzel.* / There is (we have) Wiener
>   Schnitzel (veal cutlet) today.
> *Es gibt nichts zu tun hier.* / There is nothing to do here.
> *Es gibt einen Brief für dich.* / There is a letter for you.
> *Was gibt es heute zum Abendessen?* / What is there for
>   dinner tonight?
> *So etwas gibt es nicht.* / There is no such thing.
> *Das gab es nicht.* / That did not exist.

§8.6–2 Verbs Taking the Dative

The following is a partial list of verbs that take the dative
(indirect object) in German but the accusative (the direct object) in English.

antworten / to answer	*Antworte mir!* / Answer me.
begegnen / to meet	*Wir sind ihm begegnet.* / We met him.
danken / to thank	*Ich danke dir.* / I thank you.
dienen / to serve	*Er diente ihm.* / He served him.
drohen / to threaten	*Drohen Sie mir nicht!* / Don't threaten me.
entgehen / to evade	*Er entging der Strafe.* / He evaded punishment.
folgen / follow	*Sie folgte mir.* / She followed me.
gehorchen / to obey	*Das Kind gehorcht mir.* / The child obeys me.
glauben / to believe	*Meine Frau glaubt mir.* / My wife believes me.
gratulieren / to congratulate	*Ich gratuliere Ihnen.* / I congratulate you.
helfen / to help	*Wir helfen ihr.* / We help her.
imponieren / to impress	*Er imponiert mir.* / He impresses me.
passen / to fit, suit	*Das paßt mir gut.* / That suits me fine.

schaden / to hurt	*Wird mir das schaden?* / Will that hurt me?
schmeicheln / to flatter	*Schmeicheln Sie mir nicht!* / Don't flatter me.
vertrauen / to trust	*Vertrauen Sie mir!* / Trust me.
verzeihen / to forgive	*Verzeihen Sie mir!* / Forgive me.

§8.6–3 Reflexive Verbs

Reflexive verbs usually relate an action that is directed back to the subject. The reflexive verb *rasieren* (to shave oneself) is conjugated below (present tense).

ich rasiere mich / I shave (myself)	*wir rasieren uns* / we shave (ourselves)
du rasierst dich / you shave (yourself)	*ihr rasiert euch* / you shave (yourselves)
er rasiert sich / he shaves (himself)	*sie rasieren sich* / they shave (themselves)

- Reflexive verbs usually take the accusative form of the reflexive pronoun (*mich, dich, sich;* see §7.1 – 3).
- Some common reflexive verbs are listed in the table below

Infinitive	Third Person Singular
sich beeilen / to hurry	*Er beeilt sich.* / He hurries.
sich erholen / to recover (from)	*Sie erholt sich (davon).* / She recovers (from it).
sich erinnern / to remember	*Sie erinnert sich (daran).* / She remembers (it).
sich erkälten / to catch a cold	*Sie erkältet sich.* / She catches a cold.
sich fürchten / to fear	*Er fürchtet sich (davor).* / He is afraid (of it).
sich gewöhnen / to get used to	*Er gewöhnt sich (daran).* / He gets used (to it).

Infinitive	Third Person Singular
sich irren / to be mistaken	*Sie irrt sich.* / She is mistaken.
sich sehnen / to long (for)	*Er sehnt sich (nach jemand[em]).* / He longs (for someone).
sich setzen / to sit (down)	*Er setzt sich.* / He sits down.
sich verirren / to get lost	*Er verirrt sich.* / He gets lost.
sich wundern / to be surprised	*Sie wundert sich (darüber).* / She is surprised (about it).

EXAMPLES:

Beeile dich! Es ist spät. / Hurry up. It is late.

Er erinnert sich an ihren Geburtstag. / He remembers her birthday.

Geben Sie acht, daß Sie sich nicht erkälten. / Be careful that you don't catch cold.

Setzen Sie sich, bitte! / Sit down, please.

Wir haben uns in den Bergen verirrt. / We lost our way in the mountains.

Ich wundere mich über seine Dummheit. / I am surprised at his stupidity.

Reflexive verbs taking the dative reflexive pronoun:

EXAMPLES:

Ich kaufe mir ein Buch. / I buy (myself) a book.

Du kaufst dir ein Buch. / You buy (yourself) a book.

Er kauft sich ein Buch. / He buys (himself) a book.

Wir kaufen uns ein Buch. / We buy (ourselves) a book.

Ihr kauft euch ein Buch. / You buy (yourselves) a book.

Sie kaufen sich ein Buch. / They buy (themselves) a book.

Infinitive	Example
sich etwas holen	*Hol mir die Zeitung!* / Get the paper.
sich Sorgen machen	*Mach dir keine Sorgen!* / Don't worry.
sich etwas verbitten	*Das verbitte ich mir.* / I won't stand for that.
sich etwas vergönnen	*Heute vergönne ich mir das.* / Today I'll treat myself to this.
sich wehtun	*Ich habe mir wehgetan.* / I hurt myself.
sich den Hut aufsetzen	*Er setzt sich den Hut auf.* / He puts on his hat.

Infinitive	Example
sich die Zähne putzen	*Er putzt sich die Zähne.* / He brushes his teeth.
sich das Haar waschen	*Er wäscht sich das Haar.* / He washes his hair.

Note: in reference to articles of clothing and parts of the body, the German differs from the English (see the last three sentences in the table above).

§8.6–4 Separable Prefixes

Separable prefixes can stand alone as words in their own right. They are usually removed from the verb in the present and the past tense and put at the end of the sentence.

The following table contains some of the more common verbs with separable prefixes.

Separable Prefix	Infinitive	Example
ab / off	*abnehmen* / to take off	*Er nimmt den Hut ab.* / He takes off the hat.
an / at, on	*anfangen* / to begin	*Fangen Sie an!* / Begin.
auf / up	*aufmachen* / to open	*Machen Sie die Tür auf!* / Open the door.
aus / out	*ausgehen* / to go out	*Wir gehen aus.* / We go out.
bei / by, with, at	*beitragen* / to contribute	*Er trägt dazu bei.* / He contributes to it.
ein / in, into	*einladen* / to invite	*Sie laden uns ein.* / They invite us.
fort / away	*fortgehen* / to go away	*Gehen wir fort!* / Let's go away.
heim / home	*heimkehren* / to return	*Sie kehrte heim.* / She returned home.

Separable Prefix	Infinitive	Example
herein / in, into	*hereinkommen /* to come in	*Kommen Sie herein! /* Come in.
hinunder / down	*hinuntergehen /* to go down	*Gehen Sie hinunter. /* Go down.
mit / with	*mitnehmen /* to take along	*Sie nahm es mit. /* She took it along.
nach / after	*nachdenken /* to think about	*Ich werde darüber nachdenken. /* I'll think about it
nieder / down	*niederfallen /* to fall down	*Er fiel nieder. /* He fell down.
vor / before	*vorhaben /* to have in mind	*Was hast du vor? /* What do you have in mind?
weg / away	*wegnehmen /* to take away	*Er nahm es weg. /* He took it away.
zu / to	*zugeben /* to admit	*Sie gab es zu. /* She admitted it.
zurück / back	*zurückfahren /* to drive back	*Er fuhr zurück. /* He drove back.

In tenses other than the present and the past, the verb and the prefix are not separated. In the present perfect, past perfect, and future perfect, *-ge-* is inserted between the prefix and the verb. In a dependent clause there is no separation either.

Future Tense
Ich werde heute ausgehen. / I will go out today.
Present Perfect, Past Perfect
Sie haben uns eingeladen. / They invited us.
Er war heimgekehrt. / He had returned.
Dependent Clause
Sie war dort, als er niederfiel. / She was there when he fell down.

§8.6–5 Inseparable Prefixes

The prefixes *be-*, *emp-*, *ent-*, *er-*, *ver-*, and *zer-* are inseparable from their verbs. The past participle *does not* take the prefix *ge-*. Inseparable prefixes are never stressed.

Here are some of the more common verbs with inseparable prefixes.

*be*halten / to keep	*Er hat sein Geld behalten.* / He kept his money.
*be*kommen / to get	*Er wird es bekommen.* / He will get it.
*emp*fangen / to receive	*Sie empfing ein gutes Gehalt.* / She received a good salary.
*emp*fehlen / to recommend	*Ich kann ihn bestens empfehlen.* / I can recommend him very highly.
*ent*decken / to discover	*Kolumbus hat Amerika entdeckt.* / Columbus discovered America.
*er*reichen / to achieve	*Er hat es erreicht.* / He achieved it.
*ver*kaufen / to sell	*Wir haben es verkauft.* / We sold it.
*ver*mieten / to rent	*Er hat es ihm vermietet.* / He rented it to him.
*ver*stehen / to understand	*Er hat mich verstanden.* / He understood me.
*ver*sagen / to fail	*Hat er versagt?* / Did he fail?
*zer*stören / to destroy	*Der Krieg zerstörte alles.* / The war destroyed everything.

§8.7 PRESENT PARTICIPLE

The *present participle* (the equivalent of the English verbal noun, or gerund) is formed by adding *-d* to the infinitive:

Infinitive: *singen* / to sing
Present Participle: *singend* / singing

> Note: There are two exceptions: the present participle
> of *sein* is *seiend* (being); the present participle of *tun*
> is *tuend* (doing).

When the present participle is used as an adjective, it takes
the same endings as an adjective.

der studierende Junge / the studying boy
das schlafende Kind / the sleeping child
die wachsenden Gefahren / the growing dangers

When the present participle is used as an adverb, it has no
declension.

Der Film war überraschend gut. / The film was surprisingly good.
Es hat dauernd geschneit. / It has been snowing constantly.

Here are a few examples of the present participle used as a
noun:

Dieses Hotel ist hauptsächlich für Reisende. / This hotel is
mainly for traveling salesmen.
Den Fliehenden muß man helfen. / One must help those who
are fleeing.
Weck die Schlafenden nicht auf! / Don't wake those who are
sleeping.

§8.8 MODAL VERBS

Modal verbs do not describe an action but an attitude
toward it. A modal verb is normally followed by an infinitive.

*Ich **muß** gehen.* / I must go.
*Ich **darf** gehen.* / I may go.

There are six modal verbs in German:

> *können* / to be able to, to be capable of, could
> *dürfen* / to be allowed to, may
> *müssen* / to have to, to be obliged to, must
> *mögen* / to like to, may
> *sollen* / to be supposed to, should
> *wollen* / to want to, to wish to

KÖNNEN / TO BE ABLE TO, TO BE CAPABLE OF, COULD	
Present Tense	**Past Tense**
ich kann / I can	*ich konnte* / I could
du kannst / you can	*du konntest* / you could
er kann / he can	*er konnte* / he could
wir können / we can	*wir konnten* / we could
ihr könnt / you can	*ihr konntet* / you could
sie können / they can	*sie konnten* / they could

EXAMPLES:

Ich kann gut schwimmen. / I can swim well.
Wir können nach Bonn fliegen. / We can fly to Bonn.
Er konnte Deutsch sprechen. / He could speak German.
Du kannst das machen. / You are able to do that.
Das kann nicht passieren. / That cannot happen.
Ihr könnt Bridge spielen. / You can play bridge.
Kann sie zu Hause bleiben? / Can she stay at home?
Kann er das tun? / Is he capable of doing that?
Konnten Sie ihm helfen? / Were you able to help him?
Konnte sie kommen? / Could she come?

DÜRFEN / TO BE ALLOWED TO, MAY	
Present Tense	**Past Tense**
ich darf / I may	*ich durfte* / I was allowed to
du darfst / you may	*du durftest* / you were allowed to
er darf / he may	*er durfte* / he was allowed to
wir dürfen / we may	*wir durften* / we were allowed to
ihr dürft / you may	*ihr durftet* / you were allowed to
sie dürfen / they may	*sie durften* / they were allowed to

EXAMPLES:

Du darfst ins Theater gehen. / You are allowed to (may) go to the theater.

Ihr durftet spielen. / You were allowed to play.

Sie darf Gefrorenes essen. / She may eat ice cream.

Die Kinder dürfen spielen. / The children may play.

Sie durfte nicht ausgehen. / She was not allowed to go out.

Wir durften hier rauchen. / We were allowed to smoke here.

Dürft ihr hierbleiben? / Are you allowed to stay here?

Dürfen wir mitkommen? / May we come along?

Darf ich Sie begleiten? / May I accompany you?

Durftest du ihn sehen? / Were you allowed to see him?

MÜSSEN / TO HAVE TO, TO BE OBLIGED TO, MUST

Present Tense	Past Tense
ich muß / I must	*ich mußte* / I had to
du mußt / you must	*du mußtest* / you had to
er muß / he must	*er mußte* / he had to
wir müssen / we must	*wir mußten* / we had to
ihr müßt / you must	*ihr mußtest* / you had to
sie müssen / they must	*sie mußten* / they had to

EXAMPLES:

Ich muß nach Hause gehen. / I have to (must) go home.

Sie müssen jetzt studieren. / They have to (must) study now.

Mußtest du weggehen? / Did you have to go away?

Er muß jetzt aufstehen. / He has to (must) get up now.

Wir mußten Klavier spielen. / We had to play the piano.

Sie mußte Peter abholen. / She had to pick up Peter.

Mußtet ihr lange warten? / Did you have to wait long?

Was müssen wir noch tun? / What else do we have to do?

Müßt ihr ihm zuhören? / Do you have to listen to him?

Mußt du so viel essen? / Do you have to eat so much?

MÖGEN / TO LIKE, MAY	
Present Tense	**Past Tense**
ich mag / I like	*ich mochte* / I liked
du magst / you like	*du mochtest* / you liked
er mag / he likes	*er mochte* / he liked
wir mögen / we like	*wir mochten* / we liked
ihr mögt / you like	*ihr mochtet* / you liked
sie mögen / they like	*sie mochten* / they liked

EXAMPLES:

Ich mag ihn nicht. / I don't like him.
Er mag 50 Jahre alt sein. / He may (might) be 50 years old.
Wir mochten keinen Kaffee. / We did not like (want) any coffee.
Das mag wohl sein. / That may well be.
Er mochte sie nicht. / He did not like her.
Sie mag das nicht hören. / She doesn't like to hear that.
Magst du Wein oder Bier? / Do you like wine or beer?
Mögt ihr ihn nicht? / Don't you like him?
Mögen Sie klassische Musik? / Do you like classical music?
Mochten Sie nicht das Brot? / Didn't you like the bread?

Note: *Mögen* is used mostly in a negative sense.

SOLLEN / TO BE TO, BE SUPPOSED TO, OUGHT TO, SHOULD	
Present Tense	**Past Tense**
ich soll / I am to (I should)	*ich sollte* / I should (have)
du sollst / you are to (you should)	*du solltest* / you should (have)
er soll / he is to (he should)	*er sollte* / he should (have)
wir sollen / we are to (we should)	*wir sollten* / we should (have)
ihr sollt / you are to (you should)	*ihr solltet* / you should (have)
sie sollen / they are to (they should)	*sie sollten* / they should (hav

EXAMPLES:

sollte sie besucht haben. / He should have visited her.

sollst höflich sein. / You ought to be polite.

soll reich sein. / He is supposed to be rich.

sollte ihm schreiben. / I ought to (should) write him.

Ursula soll in Wien sein. / Ursula is supposed to be in Vienna

sollt euch schämen! / You should be ashamed of
yourselves.

Wann sollen wir dort sein? / When are we supposed to be
there?

Soll ich ihn anrufen? / Shall I call him?

Soll er sich entschuldigen? / Is he to apologize?

Sollten wir ihn unterstützen? / Ought we to support him?

WOLLEN / TO WANT TO, TO WISH TO	
Present Tense	**Past Tense**
ich will / I want to	*ich wollte* / I wanted to
du willst / you want to	*du wolltest* / you wanted to
er will / he wants to	*er wollte* / he wanted to
wir wollen / we want to	*wir wollten* / we wanted to
ihr wollt / you want to	*ihr wolltet* / you wanted to
sie wollen / they want to	*sie wollten* / they wanted to

EXAMPLES:

Was wollen Sie heute machen? / What do you want to do today?

Willst du mir helfen? / Do you want to help me?

Wollten Sie hierbleiben? / Did you wish to stay here?

Wir wollen jetzt studieren. / We want to study now.

Sie will das Buch lesen. / She wants to read the book.

Ich will das nicht tun. / I do not wish to do that.

Wollt ihr ins Kino gehen? / Do you want to go to the movies?

Will er nach Berlin fliegen? / Does he want to fly to Berlin?

Wolltest du ihn besuchen? / Did you want to call on him?

Was wollte sie ihm sagen? / What did she want to tell him?

- The future tense of modal verbs is formed by using a for of *werden,* the infinitive of the main verb, plus the infinitiv of the modal verb—a construction that is called the *dou infinitive.*

  EXAMPLES:
  Ich werde nach Hause gehen müssen. / I will have to go hor
  Er wird es nicht schreiben können. / He won't be able to wri
  Sie werden nicht kommen dürfen. / They won't be allowed t
  come.

- Similarly, the present perfect (and past perfect) of modal verbs is formed with a form of *haben,* the infinitive of the main verb, plus the infinitive of the modal verb.

  EXAMPLES:
  Ich habe nicht schwimmen können. / I have not been able (I was not able) to swi
  Wir haben das Kind sehen müssen. / We had to see the chil
  Er hatte nicht rauchen dürfen. / He had not been (was not) allowed to smoke.

- There are two forms for the past participle of modal verb in German. One is identical to the infinitive:

  Er hatte nicht rauchen dürfen. / He had not been (was not) allowed to smoke.

- The other, when used in a sentence without the main ve is formed with the prefix *ge-,* just like any other verb:

  gekonnt, gedurft, gemußt, gemocht, gesollt, gewollt

  EXAMPLES:
  Ich kann Spanisch. / I know Spanish.
  Ich hatte Deutsch gekonnt. / I had known German.

  The use of *können* as a transitive verb meaning *"to know"* is limited mostly to subjects of learning, such a languages.

Er darf es nicht. / He is not allowed to do it.
Sie durfte es nicht. / She was not allowed to do it.
Wir müssen nach Hause. / We must (have to) go home.
Wir haben nach Hause gemußt. / We had to go home.
Ich mag keinen Spinat. / I don't like spinach.
Ich habe ihn nicht gemocht. / I did not like him.
Er soll das nicht. / He should not do it.

Er hat das nicht gesollt. / He was not supposed to do this.
Sie will nach Amerika. / She wants to go to America.
Sie hat nach Amerika gewollt. / She wanted to go to America.

Note: In the examples above, the main verb is understood: *Er darf es nicht (tun). Wir müssen nach Hause (gehen). Ich mag keinen Spinat (essen). Er soll das nicht (tun). Sie will nach Amerika (gehen).* Therefore, it can be omitted.

Other double infinitive constructions are used with the verbs *sehen* (to see), *hören* (to hear), and *helfen* (to help).

EXAMPLES:

Ich sehe sie kommen. / I see her coming.
Ich habe sie kommen sehen. / I saw her coming.
Ich höre ihn sprechen. / I hear him talking.
Ich habe ihn sprechen hören. / I heard him talking.
Ich helfe ihm das Radio reparieren. / I help him repair the radio.
Ich habe ihm das Radio reparieren helfen.

OR

Ich habe ihm geholfen, das Radio zu reparieren. / I helped him repair the radio.

§8.9 THE PASSIVE VOICE

§8.9–1 Present Tense

In the *active voice*—the form that we have been dealing with up to now—the subject brings about the action represented by the verb. In the *passive voice*, the subject is passive: it is being acted upon.

Active Voice
Karl füttert den Vogel. / Karl feeds the bird.
Passive Voice
Der Vogel wird von Karl gefüttert. / The bird is being fed by Ka

The agent (Karl) can also be omitted in the passive senten

Der Vogel wird gefüttert. / The bird is being fed.

In the passive voice we use a form of the auxiliary verb
werden and the past participle of the main verb. The direc
object in the original sentence *(Vogel)* now becomes the
subject. The former subject or agent *(Karl)* becomes the
object of the preposition *von (von Karl),* taking the dative.

- If the agent in the passive sentence is a living being, we u
  von. If the agent is the means by which something is done
  it becomes the object of the preposition *durch,* taking the
  accusative. This is especially true in the case of imperson
  forces (fire, flood, storm, rain, etc).

  EXAMPLES:
  Active Voice
  Der Sturm entwurzelt die Bäume. / The storm uproots the tre
  Passive Voice
  Die Bäume werden durch den Sturm entwurzelt. / The trees a
  being uprooted by the storm.
  Active Voice
  Der Mann repariert den Eisschrank. / The man repairs the
  refrigerator.
  Passive Voice
  Der Eisschrank wird von dem Mann repariert. / The refrigerat
  is being repaired by the man.

- Many intransitive verbs that take the dative (indirect objec
  such as *antworten* (to answer), *danken* (to thank), *gehor-
  chen* (to obey), *helfen* (to help), and *verzeihen* (to forgive)
  can be used in the passive voice (see §8.6-2).

  EXAMPLES:
  Der Lehrer antwortet den Schülern. / The teacher answers th
  pupils.

Dem Lehrer wird von den Schülern geantwortet. / The teacher
  is being answered by the pupils.
Die Mutter verzeiht ihrem Sohn. / The mother forgives her son.
Dem Sohn wird von seiner Mutter verziehen. / The son is being
  forgiven by his mother.
Er hilft mir. / He helps me.
Mir wird von ihm geholfen. / I am being helped by him.

§8.9-2 Past Tense

The past tense is formed from the past tense of *werden*
(wurde) plus the past participle of the main verb.

Ich wurde gesehen / I was seen.	*Wir wurden gesehen.* / We were seen.
Du wurdest gesehen. / You were seen.	*Ihr wurdet gesehen.* / You were seen.
Er wurde gesehen. / He was seen.	*Sie wurden gesehen.* / They were seen.

EXAMPLES:

Ich sah meinen Freund. / I saw my friend.
Mein Freund wurde von mir gesehen. / My friend was seen by me.
Bomben zerstörten die Stadt. / Bombs destroyed the city.
Die Stadt wurde durch Bomben zerstört. / The city was
  destroyed by bombs.

§8.9-3 Present Perfect Tense

The present perfect tense is formed from the present tense
of *sein*, plus the past participle of the main verb, plus
worden (not *geworden*).

Ich bin besucht worden. / I have been (was) visited.	
Du bist besucht worden. / You have been (were) visited.	
Er ist besucht worden. / He has been (was) visited.	
Wir sind besucht worden. / We have been (were) visited.	
Ihr seid besucht worden. / You have been (were) visited.	
Sie sind besucht worden. / They have been (were) visited.	

EXAMPLES:

Ich habe Karl besucht. / I (have) visited Karl.

Karl ist von mir besucht worden. / Karl has been (was) visited by me.

Eine Seuche hat das Volk getötet. / An epidemic (has) killed the people.

Das Volk ist durch eine Seuche getötet worden. / The people have been (were) killed by an epidemic.

§8.9–4 Past Perfect Tense

The *past perfect tense* is formed from the past tense of *sein,* plus the past participle of the main verb, plus *worden.*

> *Ich war behandelt worden.* / I had been treated.
> *Du warst behandelt worden.* / You had been treated.
> *Er war behandelt worden.* / He had been treated.
> *Wir waren behandelt worden.* / We had been treated.
> *Ihr wart behandelt worden.* / You had been treated.
> *Sie waren behandelt worden.* / They had been treated.

EXAMPLES:

Dr. Müller hatte mich behandelt. / Dr. Müller had treated me.

Ich war von Dr. Müller behandelt worden. / I had been treated by Dr. Müller.

§8.9–5 Future Tense

The future tense is formed from the present tense of *werden,* plus the past participle of the main verb, plus *werden.*

> *Ich werde gefunden werden.* / I will be found.
> *Du wirst gefunden werden.* / You will be found.
> *Er wird gefunden werden.* / He will be found.
> *Wir werden gefunden werden.* / We will be found.
> *Ihr werdet gefunden werden.* / You will be found.
> *Sie werden gefunden werden.* / They will be found.

EXAMPLES:

Karl wird das Buch finden. / Karl will find the book.
Das Buch wird von Karl gefunden werden. / The book will be
found by Karl.

§8.9–6 Modal Auxiliaries

Modal auxiliary verbs (*können, dürfen, müssen, mögen,
sollen, wollen* [see §8.8]) have no passive voice, but they
can be followed by a passive infinitive (*kann werden, soll
werden, muß werden,* etc.).

EXAMPLES:

Das kann getan werden. / That can be done.
Die Rechnungen müssen bezahlt werden. / The bills must be paid.
Die Ware sollte verkauft worden sein. / The merchandise should
have been sold.

§8.9–7 Substitutes for the Passive Voice

The passive voice is used less frequently in German than it
is in English. Sentences in the active voice using the word
man (the impersonal "one") or reflexive verb constructions
can be used instead.

EXAMPLES:

Man glaubt, daß . . . / It is believed that . . . (One believes
that . . .)
Das tut man hier nicht. / That is not done here. (One does not
do that here.)
Wie spricht man das aus? / How is that pronounced?
Man weiß, daß er reich ist. / He is believed to be rich.
Man sah ihn ins Theater gehen. / He was seen entering the theater.
Das versteht sich von selbst. / That is understood.
Das lernt sich schnell. / That is quickly (to be) learned.
Das sagt sich leicht. / That is easily said.
Das läßt sich arrangieren. / That can be arranged.

§8.9–8 The False Passive

The true passive is always formed with *werden* and the past participle of the main verb; it expresses an ongoing action. The false, or apparent, passive is formed with the verb *sein* and the past participle; it expresses the *result* of an action.

*Die Tür **wird** geschlossen.* / The door is being closed (true passive).

*Die Tür **ist** geschlossen.* / The door is closed (false passive).

In the second sentence the past participle *(geschlossen)* functions as an adjective.

EXAMPLES:

Ongoing Action
*Die Uhr **wird** repariert.* / The watch is being repaired.

Result of an Action
*Die Uhr **ist** repariert.* / The watch is repaired.

§9.

Adverbs

Adverbs are words that modify verbs, adjectives, or other adverbs. They indicate place, time, manner, and intensity.

> *Er spricht **schnell**.* He talks fast.
> *Das Mädchen ist **sehr** hübsch.* / The girl is very pretty.
> *Sie geht **hauptsächlich** abends einkaufen.* / She goes shopping mainly in the evening.

German adverbs have no endings. Almost any German adjective can, without change, be used as an adverb. There are also many words that are adverbs only.

§9.1 ADVERBS OF PLACE

Adverbs of place indicate location or direction. They determine the place of the action.

draußen	outside
drinnen	inside
droben	up there
drüben	over there
nirgends	nowhere
überall	everywhere
unterwegs	on the way

EXAMPLES:

Draußen wartet jemand. / Someone is waiting outside.
Droben ist es zu warm. / It is too warm up there.
Ich habe drüben Verwandte. / I have relatives over there.
Das habe ich nirgends gesehen. / I have not seen that anywhere.

§9.2 ADVERBS OF TIME

> *bald* / soon
> *dann* / then
> *endlich* / finally
> *gestern* / yesterday
> *heute* / today
> *inzwischen* / meanwhile
> *schließlich* / eventually
> *sofort* / right away

EXAMPLES:
Ich komme bald. / I am coming (will come) soon.
Dann ging ich nach Hause. / Then I went home.
Inzwischen rief ich ihn an. / Meanwhile, I called him.
Er kam sofort. / He came right away.

§9.3 ADVERBS OF MANNER AND DEGREE

Adverbs of manner and degree describe the way in which a situation comes about or an activity occurs.

> *beinahe* / almost
> *bereits* / already
> *besonders* / especially
> *etwa* / maybe, about
> *ganz* / quite
> *genug* / enough
> *kaum* / hardly
> *überdies* / moreover
> *ziemlich* / pretty, rather

EXAMPLES:
Er ist beinahe gestorben. / He almost died.
Sie ist etwa vierzig Jahre alt. / She is about forty years old.
Er ist ganz zufrieden damit. / He is quite satisfied with it.
Überdies raucht er zu viel. / Moreover, he smokes too much.
Der Film war ziemlich schlecht. / The film was pretty bad.

§9.4   ADVERBS INDICATING CAUTION

> *angeblich* / allegedly
> *anscheinend* / apparently
> *offenbar* / obviously
> *scheinbar* / on the face of it
> *vermutlich* / presumably
> *wahrscheinlich* / probably

EXAMPLES:

Angeblich war er ein Spion. / Allegedly he was a spy.
Offenbar tut er das gern. / Obviously he likes to do that.
Er hat vermutlich viel Geld. / Presumably he has a lot of money.

§9.5   ADVERBS WITH SUFFIXES

Adverbs with the Suffix *-weise*

> *begreiflicherweise* / understandably
> *beispielsweise* / for example
> *beziehungsweise* / respectively
> *möglicherweise* / possibly
> *schrittweise* / step by step
> *versuchsweise* / tentatively

EXAMPLES:

Begreiflicherweise kann ich das nicht erlauben. / Understandably, I cannot permit that.
Dieser Film, beispielsweise, ist sehr gut. / This film, for example, is very good.

Wir werden das schrittweise durchgehen. / We will go through this step by step.

Adverbs with the Suffix -maßen

einigermaßen / to some extent
folgendermaßen / as follows
gewissermaßen / so to speak

EXAMPLES:

Ich stimme mit ihm einigermaßen überein. / I agree with him to
  some extent.
Er schreibt das folgendermaßen. / He writes as follows.
Wir sind gewissermaßen dafür verantwortlich. / We are respon-
  sible for it, so to speak.

§9.6 COMPARISON OF ADVERBS

Adjectives used as adverbs add *-er* in the comparative. In
the superlative they take *am,* and add *-en* to the stem of
the superlative.

Karl arbeitet schwer. / Karl works hard.
Kurt arbeitet schwerer. / Kurt works harder.
Otto arbeitet am schwersten. / Otto works hardest.

The same pattern: *am* + superlative + *-en* can also be used
for predicate adjectives:

Im Herbst ist das Wetter hier am schlechtesten. / In the fall,
  the weather here is the worst.

• The adverb *gern(e)* / gladly, willingly, is frequently used with
  a verb to denote *to like to:*

EXAMPLES:

Ich habe ihn gern. / I like him.
Ich schwimme gern. / I like to swim.
Er trinkt Wein gern. / He likes to drink wine.
Er macht es gern. / He likes to do it.
Ich helfe dir gern. / I like to help you.
Er ist dort gern gesehen. / He is welcome there.
Gern geschehen! / Don't mention it.

- The comparative form of *gern* is *lieber,* and the superlative is *am liebsten. Lieber* is translated as "(I'd) rather" or "(I) prefer"; *am liebsten* can be translated as *"like best."*

    EXAMPLES:

    Ich bleibe lieber zu Hause. / I prefer staying home.
    Ich ginge lieber ins Kino. / I would rather go to the movies.
    Er bleibt am liebsten zu Hause. / He likes best to stay at home.

§9.7 MODAL ADVERBS

Modal adverbs (also called intensifying particles) are little words that lend color and emphasis to our speech. It is difficult in most instances to find the exact English equivalent for them.

German Word	Regular Meaning	Modal Usage
also	thus, therefore	*Also bis nächste Woche!* / Till next week then. *Also fangen wir an!* / Well, let's start.
denn	for, because	*Was ist denn los?* / Well, what's the matter? *Wieso denn?* / But why?
doch	however, yet	*Sie wird doch kommen?* / She will come, won't she?

German Word	Regular Meaning	Modal Usage
ja	yes	*Komm ja nicht zu spät!* / Be sure not to be late.
noch	still, yet	*Ich habe ihn noch gestern gesehen.* / I saw him only yesterday.
nur	only	*Was können wir nur tun?* / What on earth can we do? *Sei nur vorsichtig!* / Do be careful.
schon	already	*Er kam schon am folgenden Tag.* / He came the very next day. *Das ist schon richtig, aber . . .* / That is correct, no doubt, but . . .
wohl	well	*Ob er das wohl weiß?* / I wonder if he knows that. *Er ist wohl krank.* / He probably is ill.

§10.

Prepositions

Prepositions are words that combine with other parts of speech to form phrases.

EXAMPLES:
*Brot ist **auf** dem Tisch.* / Bread is on the table.
*Er tut es **für** mich.* / He does it for me.

§10.1 PREPOSITIONAL CONTRACTIONS

Sometimes, prepositions and the definite article are combined in a single word. Here are some of the more common forms of these contractions:

> *an dem = am* / at the
> *an das = ans* / to the
> *auf das = aufs* / on the
> *bei dem = beim* / at the, by the
> *für das = fürs* / for the
> *in das = ins* / into the
> *in dem = im* / in the
> *um das = ums* / around the
> *von dem = vom* / from, of the
> *zu dem = zum* / to the
> *zu der = zur* / to the

EXAMPLES:
***Am** Abend gehen wir aus.* / In the evening we go out.
*Er steht **beim** Fenster.* / He stands by the window.
*Sie geht **ins** Haus.* / She goes into the house.
*Ich erhielt das **vom** Lehrer.* / I received that from the teacher.
*Wir gingen **zur** Schule.* / We went to school.

§10.2 USAGE

In English, the noun in a prepositional phrase remains the same regardless of the preposition it follows. In German, the noun following a preposition is always in the accusative, the dative, or the genitive case.

§10.2–1 Prepositions Taking the Accusative

Preposition	Meaning	Example
bis	until, as far as	*Er wartete bis zwei Uhr.* / He waited until 2 o'clock. *Sie fährt bis München.* / She drives as far as Munich.
durch	through, by	*Er ging durch den Park.* / He walked through the park. *Das Haus wurde durch Feuer zerstört.* / The house was destroyed by fire.
für	for	*Dieses Buch ist für ihn.* / This book is for him.
gegen	against, into, around, about	*Ich bin gegen den Krieg.* / I am against war. *Sie ist gegen den Zaun gefahren.* / She drove into the fence. *Wir hatten gegen hundert Besucher.* / We had around (about) one hundred visitors.
ohne	without	*Ich trinke Kaffee ohne Zucker.* / I drink coffee without sugar.
um	around, at	*Wir bauten eine Mauer um das Haus.* / We built a wall around the house. *Er kommt um zehn Uhr.* / He comes at ten o'clock.

§10.2−2 Prepositions Taking the Dative

Preposition	Meaning	Example
aus	out of, from, (made) of	*Er kommt gerade aus der Kirche.* / He is just coming out of church. *Herr Huber kommt aus Wien.* / Mr. Huber comes from Vienna. *Der Schmuck ist aus Silber.* / The jewelry is (made) of silver.
außer	except for, out of	*Außer meiner Schwester kenne ich niemand.* / Except for my sister, I don't know anybody. *Jetzt ist er außer Gefahr.* / Now he is out of danger.
bei	at, near, with	*Sie wohnt bei ihrer Mutter.* / She is living at her mother's. *Das Haus steht bei der Schule.* / The house is near the school. *Ich habe kein Kleingeld bei mir.* / I have no change with me.
gegenüber	across from	*Uns gegenüber ist ein Park.* / There is a park across from us.
mit	with, by	*Ich arbeite mit ihm.* / I work with him. *Er kam mit dem Schiff an.* / He arrived by boat.
nach	after, to, according to	*Nach der Schule geht er schwimmen.* / After school he goes swimming. *Morgen fliegt er nach New York.* / He flies to New York tomorrow. *Dem Wörterbuch nach ist das richtig.* / According to the dictionary this is correct.

Preposition	Meaning	Example
seit	since, for	*Seit vorigem Jahr wohnt er in Köln.* / He has been living in Cologne since last year. *Er arbeitet hier seit zwei Jahren.* / He has been working here for two years.
von	from, by, of	*Sie reist von Wien nach Salzburg.* / She travels from Vienna to Salzburg. *Das ist ein Roman von Hemingway.* / That is a novel by Hemingway. *Er ist ein Bekannter von mir.* / He is an acquaintance of mine.
zu (zum, zur)	to, at, for	*Er fährt zum Flughafen.* / He drives to the airport. *Er fuhr zur Kirche.* / He drove to church. *Wir sind zu Hause.* / We are at home. *Sie bekam das zu ihrem Geburtstag.* / She received this for her birthday.

Note: The adverbs *gegenüber* (across from) and *nach* (used in the sense of ''according to'') frequently follow the noun.

- *aus* and *von*

> When indicating origin, *aus* means that one is either a native of a particular place or has been living there for some time; *von* means one has been in transit from a particular place.

EXAMPLES:
*Herr Müller kommt **aus** Bonn.* / Herr Müller comes *from* Bonn.
*Herr Müller fuhr **von** Bonn nach Hamburg.* / Herr Müller drove
  from Bonn to Hamburg.

When getting something from a person, *von* is used;
when getting something from a place, *aus* is used.

EXAMPLES:
*Er bekam ein Paket **von** seinem Sohn.* / He received a package
  from his son.
*Dieses Paket kam **aus** Bonn.* / This package came *from* Bonn.

§10.2–3 Prepositions Taking the Dative or the Accusative

The dative is used to indicate a stable position or situation.
It answers the question *wo* / where?

EXAMPLE:
*Die Katze sitzt **auf dem** Tisch.* / The cat sits *on* the table.
*(Wo sitzt die Katze? **Auf dem** Tisch.)*

The accusative is used to indicate a direction, a destination,
or a motion toward a specific goal. It answers the question
wohin / whereto?

EXAMPLE:
*Die Katze springt **auf den** Tisch.* / The cat jumps *on*(to) the table.
*(Wohin springt die Katze? **Auf den** Tisch.)*

Here we have movement toward a specific goal: the table.

- The accusative is also used if the question is:

Über was /worüber / what about?

> *Sie sprachen **über das** Buch. / They talked about the book.*

- Sometimes the dative is used if we can discern *no particular goal or destination:*

> *Er ist die ganze Zeit **in der** Stadt herumgelaufen./ He ran around town all day.*

Prep- osition	Meaning	Preposition Taking the Dative	Preposition Taking the Accusative
an	at, by, on	*Der Student steht an der Tafel. /* The student stands at the blackboard.	*Er schreibt es an die Tafel. /* He writes it on the blackboard.
auf	on, onto	*Sie sitzt auf dem Sofa. /* She is sitting on the sofa.	*Er legt das Buch auf den Tisch. /* He is putting the book on the table.
hinter	behind	*Er steht hinter dem Haus. /* He is standing behind the house.	*Die Katze läuft hinter die Tür. /* The cat runs behind the door.
in	in, into, to	*Sie ist im (= in dem) Zimmer. /* She is in the room. *Hans ist in der Schule. /* Hans is in school.	*Sie geht ins (= in das) Zimmer. /* She walks into the room. *Hans geht in die Schule. /* Hans goes to school.
neben	beside	*Das Kind sitzt neben der Mutter. /* The child is sitting beside the mother.	*Setz dich neben den Vater! /* Sit down beside the father.
über	over (above), about	*Die Uhr hängt über dem Schreibtisch. /* The clock is hanging over (above) the desk.	*Hängen Sie die Uhr über den Schreibtisch! /* Hang the clock over the desk. *Wir sprachen über die Frau. /* We talked about the woman.
unter	under, below	*Sie liegt unter den Bäumen. /* She is lying under the trees.	*Das Kind lief unter den Baum. /* The child ran under the tree.

Prep-osition	Meaning	Preposition Taking the Dative	Preposition Taking the Accusative
vor	in front of, before, ago	*Der Wagen steht vor der Tür.* / The car is standing in front of the door. *Das geschah vor dem Jahr 1941.* / That happened before 1941. *Das geschah vor vielen Jahren.* / That happened many years ago.	*Fahr den Wagen vor die Tür!* / Drive the car in front of the door.
zwischen	between	*Das Kind sitzt zwischen dem Herrn und der Dame.* / The child sits between the gentleman and the lady.	*Setz dich zwischen den Herrn und die Dame!* / Sit down between the gentleman and the lady.

§10.2–4 Prepositions Taking the Genitive

Preposition	Meaning	Example
(an)statt	instead of	*(An)statt eines Anzugs kaufte ich einen Mantel.* / I bought an overcoat instead of a suit.
innerhalb	within	*Er kommt innerhalb einer Stunde.* / He is coming within an hour.
jenseits	on the other side of	*Die Schule ist jenseits des Flusses.* / The school is on the other side of the river.
trotz	in spite of	*Trotz des Wetters ist mir nicht kalt.* / In spite of the weather I am not cold.
um . . . willen	for . . . sake	*Um Gottes willen!* / For God's sake!
während	during	*Er schläft während des Tages.* / He sleeps during the day.
wegen	because of	*Wegen seiner Verletzung kann er nicht Tennis spielen.* / Because of his injury he cannot play tennis.

§11.

Conjunctions

Conjunctions are words that connect other words, phrases, or clauses.

An independent (or main) clause has at least one subject and one predicate and can stand by itself.

EXAMPLES:
Die Frau ist nett. / The woman is nice.
Sie ist hübsch. / She is pretty.

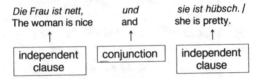

Die Frau ist nett, The woman is nice	*und* and	*sie ist hübsch.* / she is pretty.
↑	↑	↑
independent clause	conjunction	independent clause

§11.1 COORDINATING CONJUNCTIONS

Conjunctions that join words, phrases, or independent clauses of equal standing are called *coordinating conjunctions*.

The principal coordinating conjunctions are:

> *aber* / but
> *oder* / or
> *sondern* / but, rather, on the contrary
> *und* / and

Coordinating Conjunctions Joining Words

EXAMPLES:

Hans und Marie gingen ins Theater. / Hans and Marie went to the theater.

Du kannst Fleisch oder Fisch haben. / You may have meat or fish.

Sie ist dumm, aber schön. / She is stupid but beautiful.

Coordinating Conjunctions Joining Phrases

EXAMPLES:

Er geht ins Kino, aber ich nicht. / He goes to the movies, but I don't.

Sie kommt oder vielleicht ihre Schwester. / She, or maybe her sister, is coming.

Coordinating Conjunctions Joining Independent Clauses

EXAMPLES:

Alfred geht aus, und Otto bleibt zu Hause. / Alfred goes out, and Otto stays at home.

Der Vogel singt, und der Hund bellt. / The bird is singing, and the dog is barking.

Ich hörte ihn, aber er hörte mich nicht. / I heard him, but he did not hear me.

Sie ging nicht ins Kino, sondern (sie) blieb zu Hause. / She did not go to the movies but stayed at home.

Note: The coordinating conjunction *sondern* is used instead of *aber* when the preceding clause has a negative connotation, and then only when a wrong idea is replaced by a correct one.

Some conjunctions come in pairs, such as "either—or," "neither—nor." Here are some examples.

EXAMPLES:
nicht nur — sondern auch / not only — but also
Nicht nur er, sondern auch seine Frau möchte kommen. / Not

only he but also his wife wants to come.
sowohl — als auch / as well as
Sowohl er als auch sie waren hier. / He as well as she was here.
weder — noch / neither — nor
Weder Karl noch Otto ist dafür. / Neither Karl nor Otto is for it.
entweder — oder / either — or
Entweder zahlen Sie mir, oder ich verklage Sie. / Either you pay

me, or I will sue you.

Note the inversion in the first clause (verb precedes
subject) and normal word order in the second clause.

§11.2 SUBORDINATING CONJUNCTIONS

Conjunctions that make one clause dependent upon
another clause are called *subordinating conjunctions*. These
join dependent clauses to independent clauses or to other
dependent clauses. A dependent clause cannot stand by
itself.

- In English most subordinate clauses can be inverted
  without changing word order:
  When I lived in Vienna, I often went to the theater.
  I often went to the theater when I lived in Vienna.

- In German, too, the clauses can usually be inverted, but the
  word order often *does* change:
  Als ich in Wien wohnte, ging ich oft ins Theater.
  Ich ging oft ins Theater, als ich in Wien wohnte.

- Note that when the dependent clause *Als ich in Wien
  wohnte* precedes the main clause *ging ich oft ins Theater*,
  the word order changes from *ich ging* to *ging ich*.

- In dependent clauses introduced by a subordinating conjunction, the verb is at the end of the clause.

EXAMPLE:
Als er eintrat, stand jeder auf. / When he entered, everybody
got up.

or a more extensive discussion of word order, see §3.

11.2–1 The Conjunctions *wenn, wann,* and *indem* (or *dadurch daß*)

he subordinating conjunction *wenn* is used to introduce a
onditional clause.

EXAMPLE:
Wenn ich mehr Geld hätte, könnte ich mir ein Auto kaufen. / If I
had more money, I could buy myself a car.

can also imply the future.

EXAMPLE:
Wenn er zurückkommt, wird er bei uns übernachten. / When he
returns, he will stay with us overnight.

r it can express a repeated event.

EXAMPLE:
Wenn er kommt, besucht er uns immer. / Whenever he comes,
he always visits us.

ann can be a subordinating conjunction.

EXAMPLE:
Ich weiß nicht, wann er kommt. / I don't know when he will come.

* it can be an interrogative pronoun.

EXAMPLE:
Wann geht er ins Büro? / When does he go to the office?

e subordinate clause introduced by *indem* or *dadurch
β* explains the way something has been accomplished.

EXAMPLES:
Er bewies seine Freundschaft, indem er mir half.

OR

Er bewies seine Freundschaft, dadurch daß er mir half. / He proved his friendship by helping me.

- *Indem* (or *dadurch daß*) is usually expressed in English by clause starting with "by" and using the gerund (the *-ing* ending of the verb).

§11.2–2 Other Subordinating Conjunctions

Here are some other subordinating conjunctions.

als ob / as though	
bevor / before	
da / since	
daß / that	
ob / whether, if	
sobald / as soon as	
soweit / as far as	
weil / because	

EXAMPLES:
Es sah aus, als ob es regnen würde. / It looked as though it would rain.
Bevor du ausgehst, mußt du das Geschirr waschen. / Before you go out, you have to wash the dishes.
Da ich noch Zeit hatte, rief ich ihn an. / Since I still had time called him.
Ich weiß, daß sie klug ist. / I know that she is clever.
Weißt du, ob er da ist? / Do you know whether he is here?
Sobald ich ihn sehe, rufe ich Sie an. / As soon as I see him, call you.
Soweit ich informiert bin, geht es ihm gut. / As far as I know is all right.
Ich bin in die Berge gefahren, weil das Wetter schön war. / drove to the mountains because the weather was nice.

§12.

Word Formation

A most productive feature of the German language is its capacity to form new words from two or more independent words or to add prefixes and suffixes. The new word that then emerges often represents an independent unit with a meaning all its own. *Baumschule* (nursery) is not the place where trees go to school, *Handtücher* (towels) are not specifically reserved for your hands; and *Junggesellen* (bachelors) need not necessarily be young.

§12.1 COMPOUNDING INDEPENDENT WORDS

Compound nouns are produced by putting together two or more words; the last noun determines the gender and the number of the new word. The words preceding the last noun modify it. Modifying elements can be nouns, adjectives, verbs, adverbs, prepositions, and numerals. For more on compound nouns, see §4.2–3.

Nouns
der Birnbaum / the pear tree
die Landwirtschaftslehre / the agricultural science
Adjectives
der Rotfink / the bullfinch
das Gelbfieber / the yellow fever
Verbs
das Sehrohr / the telescope
die Sehnsucht / the nostalgia

Adverbs
die Jetztzeit / the present *die Wiederbelebung* / the revival
Prepositions
der Absatz / the paragraph *die Zulage* / the extra pay
Numerals
die Hundertjahrfeier / the centennial *der Dreifuß* / the tripod

- In linking compound nouns, the connecting letter *-s-* is inserted after the noun suffixes *-heit*, *-ing*, *-ion*, *-keit*, *-schaft*, *-tät*, *-tum*, and *-ung*.

  EXAMPLES:
  die Freiheitsliebe / the love of freedom
  das Lieblingsbuch / the favorite book
  die Präzisionswaage / the precision balance
  die Gesellschaftsfahrt / the conducted tour
  die Relativitätstheorie / the theory of relativity

- The connecting letters *-s-* or *-es-* follow a masculine or neuter modifying noun.

  EXAMPLES:
  der Landsmann / the compatriot
  die Tagesordnung / the agenda
  die Schiffsküche / the galley
  das Schweinsleder / the pigskin

- The connecting letter *-s-* follows a feminine modifying noun

  EXAMPLES:
  der Geburtstag / the birthday
  der Geschichtsprofessor / the history professor
  das Hilfsmittel / the remedy
  das Hochzeitsgeschenk / the wedding present

n some compounds the connecting letter -*n*- is used
following a feminine noun.

EXAMPLES:

das Eichenlaub / the oak leaves
der Scheibenwischer / the window wiper
die Sonnenfinsternis / the eclipse of the sun
der Wochentag / the weekday

§12.2 COMPOUNDING WITH PREFIXES

§12.2–1 Nouns and Adjectives

Prefix	Meaning	Examples
Ge-	Denotes a concept of collectivity.	*das Gebäck* / pastry *das Gebirge* / mountains *das Gemüse* / vegetables
Miß-	Changes the meaning of a word into its opposite. Accent is on the first syllable.	*die Mißhandlung* / maltreatment *der Mißmut* / discontent *das Mißtrauen* / mistrust
Rück-	Means going back.	*die Rückäußerung* / reply *der Rückfall* / relapse *die Rückkehr* / return *der Rückschluß* / conclusion
Un-	Indicates negation or the opposite. Sometimes also intensifies the meaning of the word.	*der Undank* / ingratitude *undankbar* / ungrateful *der Ungehorsam* / disobedience *ungehorsam* / disobedient *das Unglück* / misfortune *unglücklich* / unhappy
Ur-	Denotes origin, originality, or a primitive state.	*der Urbewohner* / native *das Urbild* / prototype *der Urzustand* / primitive state

Prefix	Meaning	Examples
Wohl-	Denotes the good, the healthy, the happy.	*das Wohlbefinden* / good health *das Wohlbehagen* / comfort *die Wohlfahrt* / welfare *das Wohlwollen* / goodwill *die Wohlstandsgesellschaft* / affluent society *wohlbekannt* / well-known *wohlerzogen* / well-bred

§12.2–2 Verb Prefixes

See §8.6–4 and §8.6–5 on the more common verbs with separable and inseparable prefixes. In this section some of the inseparable verb prefixes are discussed.

- The verb prefix *be-* turns an intransitive verb into a transitive verb.

EXAMPLES:

> *wohnen* / to live (intransitive)
> *bewohnen* / to inhabit (transitive)
> *Ich wohne in einem Haus.* / I live in a house.
> *Ich bewohne ein Haus.* / I inhabit a house.

> *weinen* / to weep (intransitive)
> *beweinen* / to mourn (transitive)
> *Ich weine über etwas.* / I weep about something.
> *Ich beweine meinen Vater.* / I weep for my father.

Here are some other verb prefixes:

Prefix	Meaning	Examples
ent-	Denotes either separation or the start of something	*entarten* / to degenerate *entblößen* / to uncover *entdecken* / to discover *enteignen* / to expropriate *entfernen* / to remove
er-	Denotes the start of something new.	*erfinden* / to invent *erforschen* / to investigate *erkennen* / to recognize *ermöglichen* / to make possible *erschließen* / to make accessible
ver-	Indicates either action in a negative sense, identification of an action, or a shift into a different state.	*verarbeiten* / to process *verarmen* / to become poor *verbergen* / to conceal *verbrauchen* / to use up *verhungern* / to starve
zer-	Indicates crushing, tearing, or breaking apart of something.	*zerbrechen* / to break to pieces *zerdrücken* / to crush *zerfallen* / to fall apart *zermahlen* / to grind down *zerreißen* / to tear up

§12.3 COMPOUNDING WITH SUFFIXES

§12.3–1 Masculine Nouns

Suffix	Meaning	Examples
el-	Often denotes tools or instruments.	*der Flügel* / wing *der Hebel* / lever *der Säbel* / sword *der Stachel* / thorn *der Schlüssel* / key

Suffix	Meaning	Examples
-er	Characterizes a person, or indicates place of origin.	der Amerikaner / American der Ansager / announcer der Bäcker / baker der Lehrer / teacher der Witwer / widower
-ling	Denotes a person's condition. Some of the words have a pejorative meaning; a few take the umlaut.	der Emporkömmling / upstart der Feigling / coward der Flüchtling / refugee der Liebling / darling der Säugling / infant

> **EXCEPTIONS:**
> die Schaufel / shovel
> die Windel / diaper

§12.3–2 Feminine Nouns

Suffix	Meaning	Examples
-e	Forms mostly abstract nouns from verbs and adjectives, often with an umlaut.	die Flechte / braid, twist die Gabe / gift die Güte / goodness die Hilfe / help die Höhe / height
-ei	Indicates places of business and occupation. Some of the words have a derogatory connotation. The accent is always on the -ei.	die Brauerei / brewery die Bücherei / library die Druckerei / print shop die Schmeichelei / flattery die Schreiberei / scribbling
-heit	Designates a condition.	die Freiheit / freedom die Kindheit / childhood die Menschheit / mankind die Schönheit / beauty die Wahrheit / truth

Suffix	Meaning	Examples
-keit	Used following the suffixes -bar, -ig, -lich, -sam, and sometimes also after -el and -er. It often denotes a character trait.	die Dankbarkeit / gratitude die Großzügigkeit / generosity die Heiterkeit / cheerfulness die Sauberkeit / cleanliness die Traurigkeit / sadness
-schaft	Indicates a condition, territory, or a collective group	die Arbeiterschaft / working class die Freundschaft / friendship die Landschaft / landscape die Ortschaft / locality, village
-ung	Denotes the consequences of an action.	die Beerdigung / burial die Erziehung / education die Genugtuung / satisfaction die Hoffnung / hope die Versicherung / insurance
-ion	Formed with nouns of foreign origin. The accent is on the last syllable.	die Lektion / lesson die Nation / nation die Revolution / revolution die Situation / situation die Station / station
-tät	Also formed with nouns of foreign origin. The accent is on the last syllable.	die Aktivität / activity die Elektrizität / electricity die Humanität / humanity die Qualität / quality die Universität / university

EXCEPTIONS:
der Glaube / belief
der Wille / will

§12.3–3 Neuter Nouns

Suffix	Meaning	Examples
-chen	This is a diminutive denoting littleness or endearment. The umlaut occurs frequently.	*das Häuschen* / little house *das Hündchen* / little dog *das Kindchen* / little child
-lein	Same as above. This suffix is less common today.	*das Brüderlein* / little brothe *das Tischlein* / little table
-nis	Denotes the result of something.	*das Ergebnis* / result *das Erzeugnis* / product *das Gefängnis* / prison *das Gelöbnis* / pledge
-sal	Results in abstract nouns.	*das Labsal* / comfort *das Schicksal* / fate *das Wirrsal* / confusion
-sel	Has a diminutive effect.	*das Anhängsel* / pendant *das Rätsel* / riddle *das Überbleibsel* / remainder
-tum	Denotes historical entities, collective units, or abstract ideas.	*das Altertum* / antiquity *das Brauchtum* / folklore *das Christentum* / Christen dom *das Eigentum* / property *das Priestertum* / priesthoo

> EXCEPTIONS:
> *die Kenntnis* / knowledge
> *der Irrtum* / error
> *der Reichtum* / wealth

§12.3–4 Adjectives

Suffix	Meaning	Examples
-bar	Denotes something that can be done or is obvious.	*fruchtbar* / fertile *sichtbar* / visible *sonderbar* / strange *unverkennbar* / unmistakable
-er	Denotes origin from a city.	*Wiener* / Viennese *Münchner* / from Munich *New Yorker* / from New York
-(e)n, *-ern*	These suffixes are used with materials.	*golden* / gold(en) *kupfern* / copper *papieren* / paper *seiden* / silk(en) *wollen* / wool(len)
-haft	Denotes the manner in which a person acts or appears to be.	*fabelhaft* / fabulous *krankhaft* / morbid *laienhaft* / amateurish *mädchenhaft* / girlish *schwatzhaft* / talkative
-ig	Denoting characterization or condition.	*findig* / resourceful *freudig* / joyful *günstig* / favorable *schmutzig* / dirty
-isch	Comparable to the English *-ish* or *-ic*, it indicates attributes, characteristics, or the place of origin.	*amerikanisch* / American *englisch* / English *musikalisch* / musical *närrisch* / foolish *tragisch* / tragic
-lich	Denotes certain qualities or characteristics.	*freundlich* / friendly *gefährlich* / dangerous *herzlich* / cordial *jugendlich* / youthful *kleinlich* / petty

Suffix	Meaning	Examples
-sam	Denotes attributes of living beings.	*arbeitsam* / industrious *fügsam* / docile *furchtsam* / timid *gemeinsam* / common *strebsam* / ambitious

Differences in meaning between adjectives ending in *-lich* and those ending in *-ig:*

geschäftlich / commercial
geschäftig / busy
mündlich / oral
mündig / of age
verständlich / comprehensible
verständig / reasonable

Differences in meaning between adjectives ending in *-lich* and those ending in *-isch:*

heimlich / secret
heimisch / domestic
kindlich / childlike
kindisch / childish
weiblich / feminine
weibisch / effeminate

12.3–5 Adjectives as Suffixes

Suffix	Meaning	Examples
-arm	Lacking in something.	*blutarm* / anemic *blutárm* / very poor *wasserarm* / lacking in water
-fähig	Able to do something.	*arbeitsfähig* / able-bodied *konkurrenzfähig* / competitive *lebensfähig* / viable
-los	Free of something (comparable to the English *-less*).	*arbeitslos* / unemployed *hilflos* / helpless *sprachlos* / speechless
-mäßig	In accordance with something.	*ebenmäßig* / well proportioned *gleichmäßig* / constant *ordnungsmäßig* / orderly
-reich	Rich in something.	*arbeitsreich* / busy *einflußreich* / influential *ereignisreich* / eventful
-voll	Full of something (comparable to the English *-ful*).	*geheimnisvoll* / mysterious *liebevoll* / affectionate *grauenvoll* / dreadful
-wert	Worth something.	*hörenswert* / worth listening to *lesenswert* / worth reading *sehenswert* / worth seeing
-würdig	Worthy of something.	*denkwürdig* / memorable *glaubwürdig* / credible *merkwürdig* / noteworthy

Special Topics

§13.

Common Phrases and Idiomatic Expressions

§13.1 COMMON PHRASES

The following turns of expression should help you in everyday conversation.

alles und nichts / all and nothing
alle zwei Tage / every other day *alles in allem* / on the whole, all told *nichts dergleichen* / nothing of the kind *für nichts und wieder nichts* / for no reason at all *Nichts zu machen!* / Nothing doing!

EXAMPLES:
Ich habe nichts dergleichen gehört. / I have heard nothing of the kind.
Alles in allem bin ich damit zufrieden. / All told, I am satisfied with it.
Er trifft ihn alle zwei Tage. / He meets him every other day.

gestern, heute und morgen / yesterday, today, and tomorrow
gestern abend / last night *heute abend* / tonight *heute morgen* / this morning *heute über eine Woche* / a week from today *morgen früh* / tomorrow morning

EXAMPLES:

Gestern abend ging ich ins Konzert. / Last night I went to the concert.
Heute morgen fahre ich nach Frankfurt. / This morning I'll drive to Frankfurt.
Morgen früh rufe ich dich an. / I'll call you tomorrow morning.

immer und nie / always and never
immer mehr / more and more
immer weniger / less and less
immer wieder / again and again
fast nie / hardly ever
nie wieder / no more, never again

EXAMPLES:

Er erzählt mir immer wieder den gleichen Witz. / He tells me the same joke again and again.
Ich habe immer weniger Lust darauf. / I feel like it less and less.
Er besucht ihn fast nie. / He hardly ever visits him.

noch / still, yet
noch immer / still
noch nicht / not yet
noch jetzt / even now
noch dazu / what's more
noch einmal / once more

EXAMPLES:

Wir sind noch immer hier. / We are still here.
Sie ist noch nicht gekommen. / She has not come yet.
Er versucht es noch einmal. / He is trying it once more.

Tag und Nacht / day and night
dieser Tage / one of these days
den ganzen Tag / all day long
Tags darauf / the day after, the next day
vergangene Nacht / last night
die ganze Nacht hindurch / all night long

EXAMPLES:

Dieser Tage werde ich sie besuchen. / One of these days I'll visit her.

Tags darauf kam er zu mir. / He came to me the next day.

Er arbeitete die ganze Nacht hindurch. / He worked all night long.

Zeit / time
auf Zeit / on credit
die ganze Zeit / all the time
Es ist höchste Zeit. / It is high time.
in kürzester Zeit / in no time
in letzter Zeit / lately

EXAMPLES:

Er kauft alles auf Zeit. / He buys everything on credit.

Es ist höchste Zeit, daß sie kommt. / It is high time that she came.

In letzter Zeit fühle ich mich nicht wohl. / Lately I don't feel well.

§13.2 IDIOMATIC EXPRESSIONS

Idioms are forms of expression in grammatical construction and phraseology that are peculiar to a people. Being unique in style and structure, they resist literal translation except in those rare instances when precisely the same idiom exists in two different languages. Idioms enrich the language and enhance its expressiveness by adding color and a distinct flavor.

Expressions with the verb *sein* (to be)

Er ist im sieb(en)ten Himmel. / He is walking on air. (He is in seventh heaven.)
Das ist mir zu hoch. / That is beyond me.
Er ist kerngesund. / He is as fit as a fiddle.

Expressions with the verb *haben* (to have)

Sie hat Grütze im Kopf. / She has brains.
Er hat die Nase voll davon. / He is fed up with it.
Er hat Geld wie Heu. / He is loaded (with money).

Expressions with the verb *gehen* (to go)

Es ging wie am Schnürchen. / It went like clockwork.
Das geht auf meine Rechnung. / This one is on me.
Er geht in die Luft. / He flies into a rage.

Expressions with the verb *kommen* (to come)

Der kommt auf keinen grünen Zweig. / He'll never make the grade.
Er kommt nicht vom Fleck. / He makes no headway.
Er kommt vom Hundertsten ins Tausendste. / He goes off on a tangent.

Expressions with the verb *liegen* (to lie)

An wem liegt es? / Whose fault is it?
Es liegt mir sehr viel daran. / It matters a great deal to me.
Das liegt mir nicht. / That's not in my line.

Expressions with the verb *machen* (to make)

Er macht gute Miene zum bösen Spiel. / He makes the best of
   a bad situation.
Mach dir nichts draus! / Don't lose any sleep over it.
Sie macht sich Luft. / She lets off steam.

Expressions with the verb *nehmen* (to take)

Er nimmt die Folgen auf sich. / He is facing the music.
Sie läßt es sich nicht nehmen . / She won't be talked out of it.
Wie man's nimmt. / That depends.

Expressions with the verb *reden* (to talk)

Er redet sich heiser. / He talks a mile a minute.
Du hast leicht reden. / It is easy for you to talk.
Darüber läßt sich reden. / That sounds reasonable.

Expressions with the verb *sagen* (to say)

Das hat nichts zu sagen. / That makes no difference.
Er hat ihm seine Meinung gesagt. / He gave him a piece of his
   mind.
unter uns gesagt / between you and me

Expressions with the verb *sitzen* (to sit)

Das sitzt ihm wie angegossen. / That fits him like a glove.
Jetzt sitzt er in der Tinte. / Now he is in the soup.
Das hat gesessen! / That hit home.

Expressions with the verb *stehen* (to stand)

Er steht in der Kreide. / He is in the red.
Es steht schlecht um ihn. / He is in a bad way.
Er steht seinen Mann. / He stands his ground.

Expressions with the verb *stellen* (to put, to place)

Wie stellen Sie sich dazu? / What do you say to this?
Er stellt sich dumm. / He plays the fool.
Er ist auf sich selbst gestellt. / He is on his own.

§13.3 MISCELLANEOUS EXPRESSIONS

The following is a short list of miscellaneous expressions that should prove useful.

---

abgesehen davon / apart from that
Einen Augenblick, bitte. / One moment, please.
Das ist ausgeschlossen. / That is out of the question.
Das ist schade. / That's a pity.
Er lernt es auswendig. / He learns it by heart.
Es steht nicht dafür. / It is not worth it.
ehrlich gesagt / frankly speaking
Das geht mich nichts an. / That's none of my business.
Gern geschehen! / Don't mention it.
Die Reihe ist an mir. / It is my turn.

EXAMPLES:
Abgesehen davon, bin ich daran nicht interessiert. / Apart from that, I am not interested in it.
Er muß das Gedicht auswendig lernen. / He has to learn the poem by heart.
Ehrlich gesagt, bin ich froh, daß er nicht kommt. / Frankly speaking, I am glad that he is not coming.
Vielen Dank für Ihre Hilfe. Gern geschehen! / Many thanks for your help. Don't mention it.
Wo spielen wir nächstens? Die Reihe ist an mir. / Where are we playing next time? It is my turn.

§14.

Numbers

§14.1 CARDINAL NUMBERS

Cardinal numbers indicate a precise quantity. They are used for counting. The numbers from zero to twenty are as follows:

Zero to Twenty			
0	*null*		
1	*eins*	11	*elf*
2	*zwei*	12	*zwölf*
3	*drei*	13	*dreizehn*
4	*vier*	14	*vierzehn*
5	*fünf*	15	*fünfzehn*
6	*sechs*	16	*sechzehn*
7	*sieben*	17	*siebzehn*
8	*acht*	18	*achtzehn*
9	*neun*	19	*neunzehn*
10	*zehn*	20	*zwanzig*

- Numbers from one to nine are called *Einer* (ones); ten, twenty, thirty, etc., are called *Zehner* (tens).
- Numbers from twenty-one on are formed by the *Einer*, followed by the word *und* (and), followed by the *Zehner:*

   einundzwanzig / twenty-one (literally, one and twenty)
   neunundneunzig / ninety-nine (literally, nine and ninety)

Twenty to One Hundred		
20	*zwanzig*	61 *einundsechzig*
21	*einundzwanzig*	62 *zweiundsechzig*
22	*zweiundzwanzig*	. . .
. . .		70 *siebzig*
30	*dreißig*	71 *einundsiebzig*
31	*einunddreißig*	72 *zweiundsiebzig*
32	*zweiunddreißig*	. . .
. . .		80 *achtzig*
40	*vierzig*	81 *einundachtzig*
41	*einundvierzig*	82 *zweiundachtzig*
42	*zweiundvierzig*	. . .
. . .		90 *neunzig*
50	*fünfzig*	91 *einundneunzig*
51	*einundfünfzig*	92 *zweiundneunzig*
52	*zweiundfünfzig*	. . .
. . .		100 *hundert (einhundert)*
60	*sechzig*	

● In numbers from 101 on, *und* is not used between hundreds (or thousands) and ones, or between hundreds (or thousands) and tens.

One Hundred to One Hundred Thousand	
100 *hundert*	1 000 *tausend (eintausend)*
101 *hunderteins*	1 001 *tausendeins*
102 *hundertzwei*	1 002 *tausendzwei*
. . .	. . .
200 *zweihundert*	1 200 *eintausendzweihundert* OR *zwölfhundert*
. . .	. . .
210 *zweihundertzehn*	100 000 *hunderttausend*
. . .	

- Groups of three digits are separated by a space. Numbers of less than one million are written as one word.

    EXAMPLES:
    dreiundsiebzigtausendvierhundertzweiundachtzig | **73 482**
    achthundertfünfundsiebzigtausenddreihundertzweiundvierzig
    875 342

Million, Billion, Trillion	
1 000 000	*eine Million*
1 000 000 000	*eine Milliarde*
1 000 000 000 000	*eine Billion*

- The German *Milliarde* is the same as the American billion; the American trillion is equivalent to the German *Billion*.

- Numbers of a million or more are not written as one word:

    zwei Millionen siebenhunderttausend | **2 700 000**

- Please note that *Million, Milliarde,* and *Billion* are feminine.

    EXAMPLES:
    London hat mehr als acht Millionen Einwohner. | London has more than eight million inhabitants.
    Das Außenhandelsdefizit der Vereinigten Staaten beträgt viele Milliarden | The foreign trade deficit of the United States amounts to many billions.

§14.1–1 The Number "One" *(ein, eins, eine)*

- The word *ein* (followed by *und*) is used to form the numerals 21, 31, etc.

    EXAMPLES:
    einundvierzig | 41
    einundachtzig | 81

The word *eins* is used to form the numerals 101, 201, 1001, etc.; it is placed at the end of the compound number and is not preceded by *und*.

EXAMPLES:

dreihunderteins / 301

zweitausendeins / 2 001

When used as a numerical adjective or pronoun, the stem *ein-* takes the same endings as the demonstrative stem *dies-* (as in *diese;* see §5.4).

EXAMPLES:

*Der **eine** Mann, den ich kannte, war nicht hier.* / The one man whom I knew was not here.

***Einer** von ihnen kam mit.* / One of them came along.

Ein does not take any endings when introducing a fraction; when preceding the noun *Uhr*, indicating time; or when followed by *oder, bis,* or *und (der-, die-) dasselbe.*

EXAMPLES:

*Er multipliziert drei Fünftel mit **ein** Sechstel.* / He multiplies three-fifths by one-sixth.

*Ich traf ihn nach **ein** Uhr.* / I met him after one o'clock.

*Die Ware kommt in **ein** oder zwei Tagen an.* / The merchandise will arrive in one or two days.

*Er muß **ein** bis zwei Monate warten.* / He must wait one to two months.

*Das ist **ein** und dasselbe.* / That is one and the same (thing).

§14.1–2 Repetitive and Duplicating Numbers

Repetitive numbers indicate how many times something is repeated. They are formed by adding the suffix *-mal* to the cardinal number.

EXAMPLES:

Ich sah ihn zweimal. / I saw him twice.

Er hat mir dreimal geschrieben. / He wrote to me three times.

- By adding the suffix -*malig* to the cardinal number, we can form adjectives: *ein-, einmalig.*

    EXAMPLES:
    Das ist eine einmalige Gelegenheit. / This is a unique opportuni‹
    Dieser Film ist etwas Einmaliges. / This film is something singula‹

- *Duplicating numbers* are adjectives that can be formed fro‹ cardinal numbers by adding the suffix -*fach.*

    EXAMPLES:
    Schreiben Sie die Rechnung in dreifacher Ausfertigung. / Writ‹
    the invoice in triplicate.
    Die Preise stiegen aufs Zehnfache. / The prices rose tenfold.

- *Zweifach* is often replaced by *doppelt* (double, twofold).

    EXAMPLE:
    Die Preise sind ums doppelte gestiegen. / The prices doubled.

§14.2 ORDINAL NUMBERS

Ordinal numbers refer to positions in a sequence or series. They are, in most cases, declined the same way as other adjectives.

der, die, das		13th *dreizehnte*
1st	*erste*	14th *vierzehnte*
2nd	*zweite*	15th *fünfzehnte*
3rd	*dritte*	16th *sechzehnte*
4th	*vierte*	17th *siebzehnte*
5th	*fünfte*	18th *achtzehnte*
6th	*sechste*	19th *neunzehnte*
7th	*siebente* (or *siebte*)	20th *zwanzigste*
8th	*achte*	
9th	*neunte*	. . .
10th	*zehnte*	
11th	*elfte*	100th *hundertste*
12th	*zwölfte*	
		. . .
		1 000th *tausendste*

Ordinal numbers written as numbers always have a period
after them.

EXAMPLES:
der 1.; der erste / the first
der 2.; der zweite / the second
der 30.; der dreißigste / the thirtieth
der 100.; der hundertste / the hundredth
Heinrich VIII.; Heinrich der Achte / Henry VIII
Elisabeth II.; Elisabeth die Zweite / Elizabeth II

Ordinal numbers are used in classifying. They indicate a
certain sequence:

1. *erstens* / first(ly) (in the first place)
2. *zweitens* / second(ly) (in the second place)
3. *drittens* / third(ly) (in the third place)

Ich sehe mir einen Film lieber im Fernsehen als im Kino an,	I'd rather watch a film on TV than on the big screen —
1. *(erstens) kostet das weniger,*	first, it costs less,
2. *(zweitens) muß ich nicht ausgehen und*	second, I don't have to go out, and
3. *(drittens) kann ich mich dabei mit meiner Frau unterhalten.*	third, I can talk with my wife while watching it.

The denominators of fractions are formed from ordinal
numbers by adding the ending *-el* to the stem of the ordinal.

$\frac{1}{3}$ = *ein Drittel*	$\frac{5}{100}$ = *fünf Hundertstel*
$\frac{1}{4}$ = *ein Viertel*	$\frac{7}{1000}$ = *sieben Tausendstel*
$\frac{3}{17}$ = *drei Siebzehntel*	

halb- (half), *Hälfte* (half), *anderthalb* (one and a half),
zweieinhalb (two and one-half).

EXAMPLES:
Sie hat den halben Kuchen gegessen. / She ate half the cake.
Die andere Hälfte gehört mir. / The other half is mine.

Ich habe anderthalb Stunden auf dich gewartet. / I waited for you for one and a half hours.

Er kommt in zweieinhalb Jahren zurück. / He will come back in two and a half years.

§14.3 MISCELLANEOUS TERMS

In German, decimal numbers are written with a comma, not a period.

> 5,6 *(fünf Komma sechs)* = 5.6
> 48,60 *(achtundvierzig Komma sechzig)* = 48.60
> 0,7 *(null Komma sieben)* = 0.7

EXAMPLES:

Das Zimmer ist 6,5 Meter (m) lang und 5,6 m breit. / The room is 6.5 meters (m) long and 5.6 m wide.

Das kostet DM 18,50. / That costs DM 18.50.

Das kostet achtzehn Mark fünfzig. / That costs eighteen marks (and) fifty (pfennigs).

Some Mathematical Expressions

der Grad / degree	*addieren* / to add
der Kreis / circle	*subtrahieren* / to subtract
das Dreieck / triangle	*multiplizieren* / to multiply
das Viereck / rectangle	*dividieren* / to divide
das Quadrat / square	

EXAMPLES:

Das Thermometer steht auf null Grad. / The thermometer is at zero degrees.

mit fünf multiplizieren / to multiply by five

durch zwei dividieren / to divide by two

A Little Arithmetic	
Sechs plus acht gleich (ist) vierzehn.	$6 + 8 = 14$
Zwanzig minus (weniger) zwölf gleich acht.	$20 - 12 = 8$
Acht mal neun gleich (ist) zweiundsiebzig.	$8 \times 9 = 72$
Dreißig geteilt durch sechs gleich fünf.	$30 \div 6 = 5$
Fünf hoch zwei (fünf Quadrat) gleich fünfundzwanzig.	$5^2 = 25$

§15.

Telling Time

§15.1 WHAT TIME IS IT?

In German you can ask this question in the following ways:

> *Wie spät ist es?*
> *Wieviel Uhr ist es?*

- When designating time, the word *Uhr* (clock) is always in the singular:

    Es ist vier Uhr. / It is four o'clock.

- The word *Zeit* (time) is not used to ask the time; it expresses an abstract concept.

    Wie die Zeit vergeht! / How time flies!
    Zeit ist Geld. / Time is money.

§15.2 THE HOURS
§15.2–1 The Twelve-Hour Clock

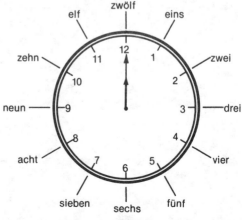

In ordinary conversation you can distinguish the different times of day by using the following expressions:

> *morgens (am Morgen)* / in the morning
> *mittags (zu Mittag)* / at noon
> *vormittags* / before noon
> *nachmittags (am Nachmittag)* / in the afternoon
> *abends (am Abend)* / in the evening
> *um Mitternacht* / at midnight
> *nachts* / at night

EXAMPLES:
Es ist sechs Uhr morgens. / It is 6 A.M.
Es ist zwölf Uhr mittags. / It is 12 P.M. (noon).
Es ist acht Uhr abends. / It is 8 P.M.

Here are some other useful phrases:

Es ist Punkt neun. / It is nine o'clock sharp.
Er trifft mich Schlag sieben Uhr. / He meets me on the stroke of seven.
Es ist ungefähr (zirka, gegen) neun Uhr. / It is about nine o'clock.

§15.2–2 The Twenty-Four Hour Clock

The twenty-four-hour clock, in German called *Bahnzeit* (railroad time), is the official time system in Germany. It is used in television and radio programs, for all public events, and for store and office hours. It is more practical than the twelve-hour system since it makes the German equivalents of A.M. and P.M. (*morgens, abends, vormittags, nachmittags,* etc.) unnecessary.

- According to German *Bahnzeit*, the hours after noon are as follows:

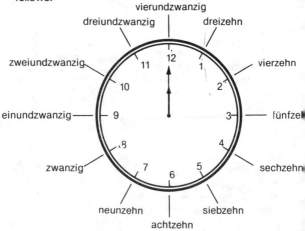

EXAMPLES:
Es ist dreizehn Uhr. / It is 1 P.M. (13:00).
Es ist sechzehn Uhr. / It is 4 P.M. (16:00).
Es ist einundzwanzig Uhr. / It is 9 P.M. (21:00).
Es ist vierundzwanzig Uhr. / It is 12 midnight (24:00).

§15.3 THE MINUTES

- Minutes *(die Minuten)* may be added directly after the hour, as in English.

    EXAMPLES:
    Es ist acht Uhr fünf. / It is eight-oh-five (8:05).
    Es ist dreizehn Uhr dreizehn. / It is thirteen-thirteen (1:13 P.M.).

Or they may be used with the word *nach* (after, past).

EXAMPLES:
Es ist zehn (Minuten) nach acht. / It is ten (minutes) past eight.
Es ist achtzehn nach sechs. / It is eighteen past six.

As the next hour approaches, you may use *vor* or *in* (to, of, before) to express minutes.

EXAMPLES:
Es ist zwölf vor elf. / It is twelve to (of, before) eleven.
Es ist fünf vor vierzehn. / It is five to (of, before) fourteen (2 P.M.).
Es ist in drei Minuten sieben. / It is three minutes before seven.

To express half and quarter hours, the words *halb* (half), *Viertel* (quarter), and *dreiviertel* (three-quarters) are used.

Es ist halb neun. / It is half past eight (literally, half [toward] nine).
Es ist halb eins. / It is half past twelve (literally, half [toward] one).
Es ist (ein) Viertel vor neun. / It is a quarter to nine.

Here *Viertel* is capitalized because it is a noun.

Es ist dreiviertel fünf. / It is a quarter to five (literally, three-quarters [toward] five).

Here *dreiviertel* is spelled with a small *d* because it is a fraction, used as an adjective.

Be careful when using *Bahnzeit*. Use hours and minutes only. Do *not* use *halb, Viertel,* or *dreiviertel*.

EXAMPLES:
Das Kino fängt um achtzehn dreißig an. / The movie starts at 6:30 P.M. (18:30).
Das Fußballspiel beginnt um fünfzehn fünfundvierzig. / The football game starts at 3:45 P.M. (15:45).

§16.

Days, Months, Seasons, Dates, and the Weather

§16.1   THE DAYS OF THE WEEK

Die Tage der Woche are:

> *der Sonntag* / Sunday
> *der Montag* / Monday
> *der Dienstag* / Tuesday
> *der Mittwoch* / Wednesday
> *der Donnerstag* / Thursday
> *der Freitag* / Friday
> *der Samstag*
>
> OR
>
> *der Sonnabend* / Saturday

Note: *Samstag* is used in Southern Germany, Austria, and Switzerland.

EXAMPLES:

Am Sonntag spiele ich Fußball. / On Sunday I will play football.
Holst du mich nächsten Dienstag ab? / Will you pick me up next Tuesday?
Ich besuche meine Schwester jeden Freitag. / I visit my sister every Friday.

16.2 THE MONTHS OF THE YEAR

Die Monate des Jahres are:

Der Januar / January	*der Juli* / July
der Februar / February	*der August* / August
der März / March	*der September* / September
der April / April	*der Oktober* / October
der Mai / May	*der November* / November
der Juni / June	*der Dezember* / December

Note: *Jänner,* instead of *Januar,* is often used in Southern Germany, Austria, and Switzerland. *Feber,* instead of *Februar,* is frequently used in Austria.

EXAMPLES:

Februar ist der kürzeste Monat des Jahres. / February is the shortest month of the year.

Im Juli oder im August geht man gern auf Urlaub. / In July or in August people like to take their vacation.

Im November ist es meistens kalt und regnerisch. / In November it is cold and rainy most of the time.

16.3 THE SEASONS

Die Jahreszeiten are:

der Frühling (das Frühjahr) / spring
der Sommer / summer
der Herbst / autumn
der Winter / winter

EXAMPLES:

Im Frühling nächsten Jahres fliege ich nach Europa. / In the spring of next year I'll fly to Europe.

Im Sommer ist es sehr heiß in New York. / In the summer it is
   very hot in New York.
*Der Herbst ist die schönste Jahreszeit im Westen der Vereinig
   ten Staaten.* / Fall is the most beautiful season in the wester
   United States.

§16.4 RELATED EXPRESSIONS

Days
am Tag darauf / the day after
den ganzen Tag / all day long
gestern abend / last night
vorgestern / the day before yesterday
übermorgen / the day after tomorrow

EXAMPLES:
Er arbeitete den ganzen Tag. / He worked all day long.
Übermorgen bin ich in Wien. / The day after tomorrow I'll be
   Vienna.

Months
alle paar Monate / every few months
Ende des Monats / at the end of the month
vorigen Monat / last month

EXAMPLES:
Wir besuchen ihn alle paar Monate. / We visit him every few
   months.
Ende des Monats haben wir meistens kein Geld. / At the end
   the month we usually don't have any money.
Vorigen Monat war ich sehr beschäftigt. / Last month I was
   very busy.

Miscellaneous
auf Jahre hinaus / for years to come
bis auf weiteres / for the present
bis vor kurzem / until recently
im Handumdrehen / in no time
über kurz oder lang / sooner or later
vorläufig / for the time being

EXAMPLES:

Bis auf weiteres brauche ich nichts. / For the present I do not
need anything.

Er macht das im Handumdrehen. / He does it in no time.

Vorläufig bin ich zufrieden. / For the time being, I am satisfied.

§16.5 DATES

For dates use the ordinal numbers, followed by the month
and the year.

EXAMPLES:

*3. Juni 1986 (der dritte Juni [am dritten Juni] neunzehnhundert-
sechsundachtzig)* / June 3, 1986

Welches Datum ist heute? / What's the date today?

Heute ist der achtzehnte November. / Today is the eighteenth
of November.

Er fährt am ersten Juli weg. / He will leave on July first.

Dates in a letter may be written in several ways:

Bonn, am 15. August 1986

OR

Bonn, den 15. August 1986

OR

Bonn, 15.8.1986 / Bonn, August 15, 1986

Note that in German the day precedes the month.

• Roman numerals are sometimes used in designating the month, mainly in business correspondence.

> EXAMPLE:
> *Ich bestätige hiermit den Erhalt Ihres Schreibens vom 14. 3. 8* *(14. III. 86)* / I confirm herewith the receipt of your letter of March 14, 1986.

• Years are usually preceded by the words *im Jahre* (in the year), but *im Jahre* can be omitted.

> EXAMPLES:
> *Er wurde im Jahre 1950 geboren.*
>
> OR
>
> *Er wurde 1950 geboren.* / He was born in 1950.
>
> *Kolumbus entdeckte Amerika 1492.*
>
> OR
>
> *Kolumbus entdeckte Amerika im Jahre 1492.* / Columbus discovered America in 1492.

§16.6 THE WEATHER

Wie ist das Wetter? / How's the weather?
Könnte nicht besser sein. / Couldn't be better.
Es ist wunderbar. / It's wonderful.
Es ist miserabel. / It's miserable.
Es regnet Bindfäden. / It's raining cats and dogs.
Es donnert und blitzt. / There's thunder and lightning.
Es ist wahnsinnig heiß. / It is terribly hot.
Es ist eine Bärenkälte. / It is dreadfully cold.
Heute hat es gehagelt. / It hailed today.
Morgen wird es schneien. / It will snow tomorrow.

Der Wetterbericht / The weather forecast
die Temperatur / temperature
die Bewölkung / cloudiness
die Feuchtigkeit / humidity
der Niederschlag / precipitation
der Wolkenbruch / cloudburst
der Schneesturm / blizzard, snowstorm
das Hochdruckgebiet / high-pressure area

EXAMPLES:

Der Himmel ist teilweise bewölkt. / The sky is partly cloudy.

Die Feuchtigkeit liegt über dem Durchschnitt. / The humidity is above average.

Der Schneesturm über Bayern dauert schon drei Tage. / The blizzard over Bavaria is in its third day.

Über dem Rheinland ist ein Hochdruckgebiet. / There is a high-pressure area over the Rhineland.

§17.

Synonyms and Antonyms

§17.1 SYNONYMS

Synonyms are words having the same or nearly the same meaning. They allow you to say the same thing in a slightly different way.

English Word(s)	German Synonyms
to admire	*bewundern, verehren, hochschätzen*
again	*wieder, nochmals, von neuem*
to aid	*helfen, unterstützen, beistehen*
although	*obwohl, obgleich, obschon*
angry	*ungehalten, aufgebracht, böse*
to answer	*antworten, erwidern, entgegnen*
anxious	*ängstlich, besorgt, bekümmert*
brave	*tapfer, mutig, unerschrocken*
complete	*komplett, vollkommen, ganz*
cosy	*behaglich, gemütlich, bequem*
customary	*gebräuchlich, herkömmlich, üblich*
delightful	*entzückend, köstlich, reizend*
to demand	*verlangen, fordern, begehren*
foolish	*dumm, albern, närrisch*
to happen	*geschehen, passieren, sich ereignen*
hideous	*entsetzlich, abscheulich, furchtbar*
hilarious	*vergnügt, heiter, ausgelassen*
honest	*ehrlich, redlich, rechtschaffen*
to intend	*beabsichtigen, vorhaben, bezwecken*
to investigate	*untersuchen, erforschen, ergründen*
kind	*freundlich, liebenswürdig, gütig*
label	*der Zettel, die Aufschrift, das Etikett*
misery	*das Elend, die Not, der Jammer*
nasty	*ekelhaft, widerlich, garstig*
now	*jetzt, nun, gegenwärtig*
to observe	*beobachten, wahrnehmen, bemerken*
obvious	*offensichtlich, offenkundig, handgreiflich*
odd	*sonderbar, seltsam, merkwürdig*

English Word(s)	German Synonyms
pain	*der Schmerz, der Kummer, die Pein*
to permit	*erlauben, gestatten, zulassen*
pleasant	*angenehm, wohltuend, erfreulich*
probably	*wahrscheinlich, vermutlich, mutmaßlich*
really	*wirklich, tatsächlich, eigentlich*
sad	*traurig, betrübt, niedergeschlagen*
spacious	*geräumig, weit, umfangreich*
stubborn	*hartnäckig, eigensinnig, starrköpfig*
sufficient	*genügend, hinlänglich, ausreichend*
talkative	*gesprächig, geschwätzig, redselig*
trouble	*die Mühe, die Plage, die Störung*
wholesome	*zuträglich, heilsam, bekömmlich*

The verbs *wissen* and *kennen* both mean "to know," but they are used in different ways.

Wissen means to know something for a fact.

EXAMPLES:
Ich weiß, daß er reich ist. / I know that he is rich.
Ich weiß, wo er wohnt. / I know where he lives.

Kennen means "to know" in the sense of "to be acquainted with"; it refers to a person, place, or thing.

EXAMPLES:
Er kennt Herrn Müller. / He knows Mr. Müller.
Sie kennt Wien. / She knows Vienna.

§17.2 ANTONYMS

Antonyms are words of opposite meaning.

alles / all	*nichts* / nothing
alt / old	*neu* / new
anfangen / to start	*aufhören* / to finish
arm / poor	*reich* / rich
der Beginn / the start	*das Ende* / the finish
bejahen / to affirm	*verneinen* / to deny
billig / cheap	*teuer* / expensive
damals / then	*jetzt* / now
erinnern / to remember	*vergessen* / to forget
erlauben / to allow	*verbieten* / to forbid
fest / solid	*flüssig* / liquid
finden / to find	*verlieren* / to lose
fleißig / industrious	*faul* / lazy
die Frage / question	*die Antwort* / answer
früh / early	*spät* / late
gesund / healthy	*krank* / ill
groß / big	*klein* / little
gut / good	*schlecht* / bad
hart / hard	*weich* / soft
jung / young	*alt* / old
der Krieg / war	*der Friede(n)* / peace
lachen / to laugh	*weinen* / to cry
langsam / slow	*schnell* / fast
leer / empty	*voll* / full
der Morgen / morning	*der Abend* / evening
sauber / clean	*schmutzig* / dirty
die Stadt / city	*das Land* / country
der Tag / day	*die Nacht* / night
viel / much	*wenig* / little
wild / wild	*zahm* / tame

Verb Charts

In the following charts you will find fully conjugated forms of some of the more representative German verbs. Their individual conjugations are displayed from left to right.

EXAMPLE:

kaufen in the present indicative:
ich kaufe (1st person singular), *du kaufst* (2nd person singular), *er kauft* (3rd person singular), *wir kaufen* (1st person plural), *ihr kauft* (2nd person plural), *sie kaufen* (3rd person plural)

bleiben   to remain

Present Indicative:	*ich bleibe, du bleibst, er bleibt, wir bleiben, ihr bleibt, sie bleiben*
Past:	*ich blieb, du bliebst, er blieb, wir blieben, ihr bliebt, sie blieben*
Present Perfect:	*ich bin geblieben, du bist geblieben, er ist geblieben, wir sind geblieben, ihr seid geblieben, sie sind geblieben*
Past Perfect:	*ich war geblieben, du warst geblieben, er war geblieben, wir waren geblieben, ihr wart geblieben, sie waren geblieben*
Future:	*ich werde bleiben, du wirst bleiben, er wird bleiben, wir werden bleiben, ihr werdet bleiben, sie werden bleiben*
Future Perfect:	*ich werde geblieben sein, du wirst geblieben sein, er wird geblieben sein, wir werden geblieben sein, ihr werdet geblieben sein, sie werden geblieben sein*
Imperative:	*bleib, bleibt, bleiben Sie*

Present Subjunctive:	*ich bliebe, du bliebest, er blieb(* *wir blieben, ihr bliebet, sie* *blieben*
Past Subjunctive:	*ich wäre geblieben, du wärest* *geblieben, er wäre geblieben* *wir wären geblieben, ihr wär(* *geblieben, sie wären geblieb(*
Present Conditional:	*ich würde bleiben, du würdest* *bleiben, er würde bleiben, w(* *würden bleiben, ihr würdet* *bleiben, sie würden bleiben*
Past Conditional:	*ich würde geblieben sein, du* *würdest geblieben sein, er* *würde geblieben sein, wir w(* *den geblieben sein, ihr würd(* *geblieben sein, sie würden* *geblieben sein*

fallen   to fall

Present Indicative:	*ich falle, du fällst, er fällt, wir* *fallen, ihr fallt, sie fallen*
Past:	*ich fiel, du fielst, er fiel, wir* *fielen, ihr fielt, sie fielen*
Present Perfect:	*ich bin gefallen, du bist gefallen* *er ist gefallen, wir sind gefal-* *len, ihr seid gefallen, sie sind* *gefallen*
Past Perfect:	*ich war gefallen, etc.*
Future:	*ich werde fallen, etc.*
Future Perfect:	*ich werde gefallen sein, etc.*
Imperative:	*fall, fallt, fallen Sie*
Present Subjunctive:	*ich fiele, du fielest, er fiele, wir* *fielen, ihr fielet, sie fielen*
Past Subjunctive:	*ich wäre gefallen, du wärest* *gefallen, er wäre gefallen, wi(* *wären gefallen, ihr wäret* *gefallen, sie wären gefallen*

Present Conditional:	*ich würde fallen*, etc.
Past Conditional:	*ich würde gefallen sein*, etc.

kaufen to buy

Present Indicative:	*ich kaufe, du kaufst, er kauft, wir kaufen, ihr kauft, sie kaufen*
Past:	*ich kaufte, du kauftest, er kaufte, wir kauften, ihr kauftet, sie kauften*
Present Perfect:	*ich habe gekauft, du hast gekauft, er hat gekauft, wir haben gekauft, ihr habt gekauft, sie haben gekauft*
Past Perfect:	*ich hatte gekauft, du hattest gekauft, er hatte gekauft, wir hatten gekauft, ihr hattet gekauft, sie hatten gekauft*
Future:	*ich werde kaufen, du wirst kaufen, er wird kaufen, wir werden kaufen, ihr werdet kaufen, sie werden kaufen*
Future Perfect:	*ich werde gekauft haben, du wirst gekauft haben, er wird gekauft haben, wir werden gekauft haben, ihr werdet gekauft haben, sie werden gekauft haben*
Imperative:	*kauf, kauft, kaufen Sie*
Present Subjunctive:	(same as past tense)
Past Subjunctive:	*ich hätte gekauft, du hättest gekauft, er hätte gekauft, wir hätten gekauft, ihr hättet gekauft, sie hätten gekauft*
Present Conditional:	*ich würde kaufen, du würdest kaufen, er würde kaufen, wir würden kaufen, ihr würdet kaufen, sie würden kaufen*

Past Conditional:	*ich würde gekauft haben, du würdest gekauft haben, er würde gekauft haben, wir würden gekauft haben, ihr würdet gekauft haben, sie würden gekauft haben*
Present Passive:	*es wird gekauft, sie werden gekauft*
Past Passive:	*es wurde gekauft, sie wurden gekauft*
Present Perfect Passive:	*es ist gekauft worden, sie sind gekauft worden*
Future Passive:	*es wird gekauft werden, sie werden gekauft werden*

kommen to come

Present Indicative:	*ich komme, du kommst, er kommt, wir kommen, ihr kommt, sie kommen*
Past:	*ich kam, du kamst, er kam, wir kamen, ihr kamt, sie kamen*
Present Perfect:	*ich bin gekommen, du bist gekommen, er ist gekommen, wir sind gekommen, ihr seid gekommen, sie sind gekommen*
Past Perfect:	*ich war gekommen, etc.*
Future:	*ich werde kommen, etc.*
Future Perfect:	*ich werde gekommen sein, etc.*
Imperative:	*komm, kommt, kommen Sie*
Present Subjunctive:	*ich käme, du kämest, er käme, wir kämen, ihr kämet, sie kämen*
Past Subjunctive:	*ich wäre gekommen, du wärest gekommen, er wäre gekommen, wir wären gekommen, ihr wäret gekommen, sie wären gekommen*

| Present Conditional: | *ich würde kommen*, etc. |
| Past Conditional: | *ich würde gekommen sein*, etc. |

lesen to read

Present Indicative:	*ich lese, du liest, er liest, wir lesen, ihr lest, sie lesen*
Past:	*ich las, du last, er las, wir lasen, ihr last, sie lasen*
Present Perfect:	*ich habe gelesen, du hast gelesen, er hat gelesen, wir haben gelesen, ihr habt gelesen, sie haben gelesen*
Past Perfect:	*ich hatte gelesen, du hattet gelesen, er hatte gelesen, wir hatten gelesen, ihr hattet gelesen, sie hatten gelesen*
Future:	*ich werde lesen*, etc.
Future Perfect:	*ich werde gelesen haben*, etc.
Imperative:	*lies, lest, lesen Sie*
Present Subjunctive:	*ich läse, du läsest, er läse, wir läsen, ihr läset, sie läsen*
Past Subjunctive:	*ich hätte gelesen, du hättest gelesen, er hätte gelesen, wir hätten gelesen, ihr hättet gelesen, sie hätten gelesen*
Present Conditional:	*ich würde lesen*, etc.
Past Conditional:	*ich würde gelesen haben*, etc.
Present Passive:	*es wird gelesen, sie werden gelesen*
Past Passive:	*es wurde gelesen, sie wurden gelesen*
Present Perfect Passive:	*es ist gelesen worden, sie sind gelesen worden*
Future Passive:	*es wird gelesen werden, sie werden gelesen werden*

sehen to see

Present Indicative:	*ich sehe, du siehst, er sieht, wir sehen, ihr seht, sie sehen*
Past:	*ich sah, du sahst, er sah, wir sahen, ihr saht, sie sahen*
Present Perfect:	*ich habe gesehen, du hast gesehen, er hat gesehen, wir haben gesehen, ihr habt gesehen, sie haben gesehen*
Past Perfect:	*ich hatte gesehen, etc.*
Future:	*ich werde sehen, etc.*
Future Perfect:	*ich werde gesehen haben, etc.*
Imperative:	*sieh, seht, sehen Sie*
Present Subjunctive:	*ich sähe, du sähest, er sähe, wir sähen, ihr sähet, sie sähen*
Past Subjunctive:	*ich hätte gesehen, du hättest gesehen, er hätte gesehen, wir hätten gesehen, ihr hättet gesehen, sie hätten gesehen*
Present Conditional:	*ich würde sehen, etc.*
Past Conditional:	*ich würde gesehen haben, etc.*
Present Passive:	*ich werde gesehen, du wirst gesehen, er wird gesehen, wir werden gesehen, ihr werdet gesehen, sie werden gesehen*
Past Passive:	*ich wurde gesehen, du wurdest gesehen, er wurde gesehen, wir wurden gesehen, ihr wurdet gesehen, sie wurden gesehen*
Present Perfect Passive:	*ich bin gesehen worden, du bist gesehen worden, er ist gesehen worden, wir sind gesehen worden, ihr seid gesehen worden, sie sind gesehen worden*

Future Passive: *ich werde gesehen werden, du
                         wirst gesehen werden, er wird
                         gesehen werden, wir werden
                         gesehen werden, ihr werdet
                         gesehen werden, sie werden
                         gesehen werden*

sich setzen   to sit down

Present Indicative: *ich setze mich, du setzt dich, er
                         setzt sich, wir setzen uns, ihr
                         setzt euch, sie setzen sich*

Past: *ich setzte mich, du setztest dich,
                         er setzte sich, wir setzten uns,
                         ihr setztet euch, sie setzten sich*

Present Perfect: *ich habe mich gesetzt, du hast
                         dich gesetzt, er hat sich
                         gesetzt, wir haben uns gesetzt,
                         ihr habt euch gesetzt, sie
                         haben sich gesetzt*

Past Perfect: *ich hatte mich gesetzt, du hattest
                         dich gesetzt, er hatte sich
                         gesetzt, wir hatten uns gesetzt,
                         ihr hattet euch gesetzt, sie
                         hatten sich gesetzt*

Future: *ich werde mich setzen, du wirst
                         dich setzen, er wird sich
                         setzen, wir werden uns
                         setzen, ihr werdet euch
                         setzen, sie werden sich setzen*

Future Perfect: *ich werde mich gesetzt haben,
                         du wirst dich gesetzt haben, er
                         wird sich gesetzt haben, wir
                         werden uns gesetzt haben, ihr
                         werdet euch gesetzt haben,
                         sie werden sich gesetzt haben*

Imperative: *setz dich, setzt euch, setzen Sie
                         sich*

Present Subjunctive: (same as past tense)

Past Subjunctive:	*ich hätte mich gesetzt, du hättest dich gesetzt, er hätte sich gesetzt, wir hätten uns gesetzt, ihr hättet euch gesetzt, sie hätten sich gesetzt*
Present Conditional:	*ich würde mich setzen, du würdest dich setzen, er würde sich setzen, wir würden uns setzen, ihr würdet euch setzen, sie würden sich setzen*
Past Conditional:	*ich würde mich gesetzt haben, du würdest dich gesetzt haben, er würde sich gesetzt haben, wir würden uns gesetzt haben, ihr würdet euch gesetzt haben, sie würden sich gesetzt haben*

sitzen   to sit

Present Indicative:	*ich sitze, du sitzt, er sitzt, wir sitzen, ihr sitzt, sie sitzen*
Past:	*ich saß, du saßest, er saß, wir saßen, ihr saßet, sie saßen*
Present Perfect:	*ich habe gesessen, du hast gesessen, er hat gesessen, wir haben gesessen, ihr habt gesessen, sie haben gesessen*
Past Perfect:	*ich hatte gesessen, etc.*
Future:	*ich werde sitzen, etc.*
Future Perfect:	*ich werde gesessen haben, etc.*
Imperative:	*sitz, sitzt, sitzen Sie*
Present Subjunctive:	*ich säße, du säßest, er säße, wir säßen, ihr säßet, sie säßen*

Past Subjunctive:	*ich hätte gesessen, du hättest gesessen, er hätte gesessen, wir hätten gesessen, ihr hättet gesessen, sie hätten gesessen*
Present Conditional:	*ich würde sitzen, etc.*
Past Conditional:	*ich würde gesessen haben, etc.*

sprechen   to speak

Present Indicative:	*ich spreche, du sprichst, er spricht, wir sprechen, ihr sprecht, sie sprechen*
Past:	*ich sprach, du sprachst, er sprach, wir sprachen, ihr spracht, sie sprachen*
Present Perfect:	*ich habe gesprochen, du hast gesprochen, er hat gesprochen, wir haben gesprochen, ihr habt gesprochen, sie haben gesprochen*
Past Perfect:	*ich hatte gesprochen, etc.*
Future:	*ich werde sprechen, etc.*
Future Perfect:	*ich werde gesprochen haben, etc.*
Imperative:	*sprich, sprecht, sprechen Sie*
Present Subjunctive:	*ich spräche, du sprächest, er spräche, wir sprächen, ihr sprächet, sie sprächen*
Past Subjunctive:	*ich hätte gesprochen, du hättest gesprochen, er hätte gesprochen, wir hätten gesprochen, ihr hättet gesprochen, sie hätten gesprochen*
Present Conditional:	*ich würde sprechen, etc.*
Past Conditional:	*ich würde gesprochen haben, etc.*

stehen to stand

Present Indicative:	*ich stehe, du stehst, er steht, wir stehen, ihr steht, sie stehen*
Past:	*ich stand, du stand(e)st, er stand, wir standen, ihr standet, sie standen*
Present Perfect:	*ich habe gestanden, du hast gestanden, er hat gestanden, wir haben gestanden, ihr habt gestanden, sie haben gestanden*
Past Perfect:	*ich hatte gestanden, etc.*
Future:	*ich werde stehen, etc.*
Future Perfect:	*ich werde gestanden haben, etc*
Imperative:	*steh, steht, stehen Sie*
Present Subjunctive:	*ich stünde, du stündest, er stünde, wir stünden, ihr stündet, sie stünden*
Past Subjunctive:	*ich hätte gestanden, du hättest gestanden, er hätte gestanden, wir hätten gestanden, ihr hättet gestanden, sie hätten gestanden*
Present Conditional:	*ich würde stehen, etc.*
Past Conditional:	*ich würde gestanden haben, etc*

es können to know it, to be able to do it

Present Indicative:	*ich kann es, du kannst es, er kann es, wir können es, ihr könnt es, sie können es*
Past:	*ich konnte es, du konntest es, er konnte es, wir konnten es, ihr konntet es, sie konnten es*
Present Perfect:	*ich habe es gekonnt, du hast es gekonnt, er hat es gekonnt, wir haben es gekonnt, ihr habt es gekonnt, sie haben es gekonnt*

Past Perfect:	*ich hatte es gekonnt, etc.*
Future:	*ich werde es können, du wirst es können, er wird es können, wir werden es können, ihr werdet es können, sie werden es können*
Future Perfect:	*ich werde es gekonnt haben, etc.*
Present Subjunctive:	*ich könnte es, du könntest es, er könnte es, wir könnten es, ihr könntet es, sie könnten es*
Past Subjunctive:	*ich hätte es gekonnt, du hättest es gekonnt, er hätte es gekonnt, wir hätten es gekonnt, ihr hättet es gekonnt, sie hätten es gekonnt*
Present Conditional:	*ich würde es können, du würdest es können, er würde es können, wir würden es können, ihr würdet es können, sie würden es können*
Past Conditional:	*ich würde es gekonnt haben, du würdest es gekonnt haben, er würde es gekonnt haben, wir würden es gekonnt haben, ihr würdet es gekonnt haben, sie würden es gekonnt haben*

es lesen können   to be able to read it

Present Indicative:	*ich kann es lesen, du kannst es lesen, er kann es lesen, wir können es lesen, ihr könnt es lesen, sie können es lesen*
Past:	*ich konnte es lesen, du konntest es lesen, er konnte es lesen, wir konnten es lesen, ihr konntet es lesen, sie konnten es lesen*

Present Perfect:	*ich habe es lesen können, du hast es lesen können, er hat es lesen können, wir haben es lesen können, ihr habt es lesen können, sie haben es lesen können*
Past Perfect:	*ich hatte es lesen können, etc.*
Future:	*ich werde es lesen können, etc.*
Subjunctive:	*ich hätte es lesen können, du hättest es lesen können, er hätte es lesen können, wir hätten es lesen können, ihr hättet es lesen können, sie hätten es lesen können*
Conditional:	*ich würde es lesen können, du würdest es lesen können, er würde es lesen können, wir würden es lesen können, ihr würdet es lesen können, sie würden es lesen können*

Strong and Irregular Verbs

Infinitive	Present Indicative	Past Tense	Past Participle	Meaning
backen	bäckt	backte (buk)	gebacken	to bake
befehlen	befiehlt	befahl	befohlen	to order
beginnen	beginnt	begann	begonnen	to begin
beißen	beißt	biß	gebissen	to bite
biegen	biegt	bog	gebogen	to bend
bieten	bietet	bot	geboten	to offer
binden	bindet	band	gebunden	to bind
bitten	bittet	bat	gebeten	to ask
blasen	bläst	blies	geblasen	to blow
bleiben	bleibt	blieb	ist geblieben	to stay
braten	brät	briet	gebraten	to roast
brechen	bricht	brach	gebrochen	to break
brennen	brennt	brannte	gebrannt	to burn
bringen	bringt	brachte	gebracht	to bring
denken	denkt	dachte	gedacht	to think
dürfen	darf	durfte	gedurft dürfen	to be permitted (may)
empfehlen	empfiehlt	empfahl	empfohlen	to recommend
essen	ißt	aß	gegessen	to eat
fahren	fährt	fuhr	ist gefahren	to travel
fallen	fällt	fiel	ist gefallen	to fall
fangen	fängt	fing	gefangen	to catch
finden	findet	fand	gefunden	to find
fliegen	fliegt	flog	ist geflogen	to fly
fliehen	flieht	floh	ist geflohen	to flee
fließen	fließt	floß	ist geflossen	to flow
frieren	friert	fror	gefroren	to freeze
geben	gibt	gab	gegeben	to give
gehen	geht	ging	ist gegangen	to go
gelingen	gelingt	gelang	ist gelungen	to succeed
geschehen	geschieht	geschah	ist geschehen	to happen
gewinnen	gewinnt	gewann	gewonnen	to win
gießen	gießt	goß	gegossen	to pour
graben	gräbt	grub	gegraben	to dig
greifen	greift	griff	gegriffen	to seize
haben	hat	hatte	gehabt	to have
halten	hält	hielt	gehalten	to hold

Infinitive	Present Indicative	Past Tense	Past Participle	Meaning
heben	hebt	hob	gehoben	to lift
heißen	heißt	hieß	geheißen	to call
helfen	hilft	half	geholfen	to help
kennen	kennt	kannte	gekannt	to know
klingen	klingt	klang	geklungen	to sound
kommen	kommt	kam	ist gekommen	to come
können	kann	konnte	gekonnt können	to be able to (could)
kriechen	kriecht	kroch	ist gekrochen	to crawl
laden	lädt	lud	geladen	to load
lassen	läßt	ließ	gelassen lassen	to let
laufen	läuft	lief	ist gelaufen	to run
leiden	leidet	litt	gelitten	to suffer
leihen	leiht	lieh	geliehen	to lend
lesen	liest	las	gelesen	to read
liegen	liegt	lag	gelegen	to lie
lügen	lügt	log	gelogen	to lie
meiden	meidet	mied	gemieden	to avoid
messen	mißt	maß	gemessen	to measure
mißlingen	mißlingt	mißlang	ist mißlungen	to fail
mögen	mag	mochte	gemocht mögen	to like to (may)
müssen	muß	mußte	gemußt müssen	to have to (must)
nehmen	nimmt	nahm	genommen	to take
nennen	nennt	nannte	genannt	to name
pfeifen	pfeift	pfiff	gepfiffen	to whistle
raten	rät	riet	geraten	to advise
reißen	reißt	riß	gerissen	to tear
reiten	reitet	ritt	ist geritten	to ride
rennen	rennt	rannte	ist gerannt	to run
riechen	riecht	roch	gerochen	to smell
rufen	ruft	rief	gerufen	to call
schaffen	schafft	schuf	geschaffen	to create
scheinen	scheint	schien	geschienen	to shine, to seem
scheren	schert	schor	geschoren	to shear
schießen	schießt	schoß	geschossen	to shoot
schlafen	schläft	schlief	geschlafen	to sleep
schlagen	schlägt	schlug	geschlagen	to beat
schließen	schließt	schloß	geschlossen	to close

Infinitive	Present Indicative	Past Tense	Past Participle	Meaning
schneiden	schneidet	schnitt	geschnitten	to cut
schreiben	schreibt	schrieb	geschrieben	to write
schreien	schreit	schrie	geschrie(e)n	to cry (out)
schweigen	schweigt	schwieg	geschwiegen	to be silent
schwimmen	schwimmt	schwamm	ist geschwommen	to swim
schwören	schwört	schwor	geschworen	to swear
sehen	sieht	sah	gesehen	to see
sein	ist	war	ist gewesen	to be
senden	sendet	sandte	gesandt	to send
singen	singt	sang	gesungen	to sing
sinken	sinkt	sank	ist gesunken	to sink
sitzen	sitzt	saß	gesessen	to sit
sollen	soll	sollte	gesollt, sollen	to be supposed to (should)
sprechen	spricht	sprach	gesprochen	to speak
springen	springt	sprang	ist gesprungen	to jump
stehen	steht	stand	gestanden	to stand
stehlen	stiehlt	stahl	gestohlen	to steal
steigen	steigt	stieg	ist gestiegen	to go up
sterben	stirbt	starb	ist gestorben	to die
stoßen	stößt	stieß	gestoßen	to push
streichen	streicht	strich	gestrichen	to stroke
streiten	streitet	stritt	gestritten	to quarrel
tragen	trägt	trug	getragen	to carry, to wear
treffen	trifft	traf	getroffen	to meet
treten	tritt	trat	ist getreten	to step
trinken	trinkt	trank	getrunken	to drink
tun	tut	tat	getan	to do
verbergen	verbirgt	verbarg	verborgen	to hide
verderben	verdirbt	verdarb	verdorben	to spoil
vergessen	vergißt	vergaß	vergessen	to forget
vergleichen	vergleicht	verglich	verglichen	to compare
verlieren	verliert	verlor	verloren	to lose
verzeihen	verzeiht	verzieh	verziehen	to forgive
wachsen	wächst	wuchs	ist gewachsen	to grow
waschen	wäscht	wusch	gewaschen	to wash
weben	webt	wob	gewoben	to weave
werden	wird	wurde	ist geworden	to become
werfen	wirft	warf	geworfen	to throw
wissen	weiß	wußte	gewußt	to know

Infinitive	Present Indicative	Past Tense	Past Participle	Meaning
wollen	will	wollte	gewollt wollen	to want to
zerreißen	zerreißt	zerriß	zerrissen	to tear apart
ziehen	zieht	zog	gezogen	to draw, pull
zwingen	zwingt	zwang	gezwungen	to force

Note: Present indicative and past tense verbs are given in the third person singular.

Index

References in this index to the Basics, the Parts of Speech, and Special Topics are indicated by the symbol § followed by the decimal number. References to verb charts are given by page (pp.) number.